COMPOSTING
for
CANADA

Suzanne Lewis

LONE
PINE

The Publisher: Lone Pine Publishing
10145–81 Avenue
Edmonton, AB T6E 1W9
Canada
Website: www.lonepinepublishing.com

Library and Archives Canada Cataloguing in Publication

Lewis, Suzanne, 1980-
     Composting for Canada / Suzanne Lewis.

Includes bibliographical references and index.
ISBN 978-1-55105-843-6

     1. Compost. 2. Gardening--Canada. I. Title.

S661.L49 2010   631.8'75   C2010-906960-1

Editorial Director: Nancy Foulds
Project Editor: Wendy Pirk
Editorial Support: Sheila Quinlan
Production Manager: Gene Longson
Book Design and Layout: Janina Kuerschner
Cover Design: Gerry Dotto

Photos: Sandra Bit 110, 145; Dreamstime 132, 150; Tamara Eder 11, 19, 27, 47, 61, 79, 80, 85, 88, 95, 99, 102, 137, 152; Jen Fafard 63; Derek Fell 55, 62, 83, 108, 122, 130; James A. Gordon 86; iStock 25, 29, 75, 76, 94, 107; Suzanne Lewis 13a&b, 17a&b, 18a&b, 21, 23, 41, 44, 46, 51, 52, 53, 114, 115, 116, 117, 118, 119, 120, 139; Tim Matheson 26, 28, 33, 34, 50, 57, 65a, 69, 90, 140a; Allison Penko 36; Laura Peters 14, 24, 65b, 72a, 73, 89, 91, 93, 97, 106, 112, 136, 142a&b, 143a, 144; photos.com 1, 31, 60, 66, 67, 68, 70, 84, 100, 154, 156, 157; Robert Ritchie 72b, 123a&b, 141; Nanette Samol 133; Soil Foodweb Inc. 6, 7a,b&c; TPI 87; Gary Whyte 131; Don Williamson 64, 135, 140b, 143b.

Illustrations: Frank Burman 8, 12, 39, 40, 45, 48–49, 96, 98, 109, 111, 126, 138, 151a&b; George Penetrante 134; Gary Ross 105, 154, 155; Ian Sheldon 64, 127, 128, 129, 149, 153.

We acknowledge the financial support of the Government of Canada through the Book Publishing Industry Development Program (BPIDP) for our publishing activities.

PC: 1

Acknowledgements

Allan Yee, for photos and wonderful information in your composting presentations.

Ken Tingley, for encouragement and composting information.

Edmonton Waste Management Branch: Connie, Garry, Karen, Rose, Mark, Anna and everyone else, for helping me with photos and sage advice.

The Master Composter Program of Edmonton, for photos and input.

My editors, Nancy Foulds and Wendy Pirk, for making my book an easy and interesting read.

Kevin, for support and encouragement at home.

My family, for believing that I could pull this off.

Suzanne Lewis

Table of Contents

Introduction

What is Composting?

Composting completes nature's cycle in your backyard by returning organic and mineral matter back to your soil. Simply put, composting is the rebirth stage of nature's cycle. Your plants consume nutrients from the dirt; when the plants die, small creatures such as bugs and bacteria consume the plants and return the nutrients back to the dirt, allowing new plants to grow and flourish.

The end product of composting is sometimes referred to as humus, which is just a fancy name for decomposed organic matter. Organic matter is made of dead plants and animals that have been consumed by the critters that live in or above the soil.

It is hard for us to resist the urge to improve on nature. We are always striving to speed up processes and increase efficiency. Such is the case with composting. Left alone, yard waste will take one to three years to decompose completely, but with a little effort, you can see finished results in one season. How much effort you put into composting determines how quickly compost is produced. If you create the right living conditions for the decomposers to thrive, and if you monitor the pile to make sure the decomposers are doing what they should, you will quickly see the results of your efforts.

The Soil Food Web

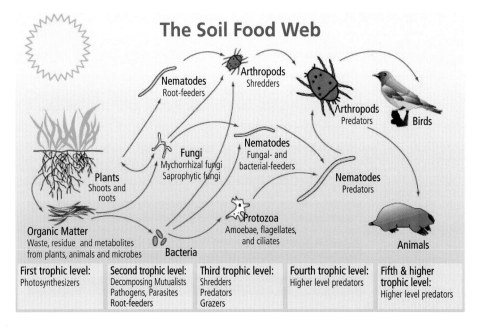

First trophic level:	Second trophic level:	Third trophic level:	Fourth trophic level:	Fifth & higher trophic level:
Photosynthesizers	Decomposing Mutualists Pathogens, Parasites Root-feeders	Shredders Predators Grazers	Higher level predators	Higher level predators

Mass of fungal strands

Although some people are determined to get finished compost as soon as possible, others are content to wait and let nature take its time. It is perfectly okay to just dig a hole, throw in some yard waste, cover it up and come back for your finished compost in a few years. Either way, composting returns those nutrients used by your plants back to the soil, renewing the lifespan of your garden.

Why Compost?

Fungal hyphae

Your compost pile is rich in organic matter and contains billions of microorganisms—organisms that can fix nitrogen from the air or can make phosphorus, iron and other important nutrients available to your plants.

A healthy garden's soil is not just dirt and mineral particles; it is an ecosystem that is home to millions of microorganisms living in a symbiotic relationship with your plants. Biological organisms in the soil feed off sweet enzymes emitted by the roots of your plants; in exchange, the microorganisms release their own enzymes and acids to increase plant growth. The mineral matter in soil anchors the plant roots in place and provides a home for the organisms that feed off the organic matter in the soil. The symbiotic relationship between plants and microorganisms is possible only through the addition of organic matter to the soil. The best way to add organic matter to the soil is through composting.

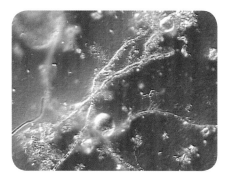

Fungi and bacteria

Composting Throughout History

Human history has a special reverence for compost. Since the beginning of agriculture, ten thousand years ago, humans have developed and used compost to increase the fertility of soil. The first compost heaps were made from manure and plant waste, and both components have remained integral in soil conditioning for farmers throughout the ages.

Historians theorize that the Chinese have been composting on a large scale since about 6000 BC—though the first written reference to composting manure is from clay tablets said to have originated in the Akkadian Empire of Mesopotamia, in modern-day Iraq, around 2400 BC. The Bible in the original Hebrew texts makes reference to dung hills, dung as fuel and dung as fertilizer. The Talmud, the ancient authoritative text of Orthodox Judaism, encouraged composting manures before incorporating them in the soil, using waste plant debris around the base of trees and using blood from animal sacrifice as a soil amendment. Knowledge of composting survived the Middle Ages, preserved in the writings

The Indore method uses traditional composting procedures and is commonly practised in countries such as India and China.

of the medieval church and in the writings of learned Arabs.

The Birth of Agricultural Chemistry

In 1834, French biologist Jean Baptiste Boussingault began what we now refer to as agricultural chemistry. Agricultural chemists look at growth and nutrients in plants on a molecular level. They develop and experiment with chemical fertilizers, herbicides and pesticides to improve crop survival and growth rates. In 1840, German chemist Justus von Liebig experimented with dissolved nutrients in water and theorized that, contrary to popular belief, plants did not need organic particles to grow. Plants are capable of absorbing nutrients dissolved in water instead. Since then, farmers have turned away from the practices of old to become increasingly dependent on chemicals for crop growth.

Von Liebig did not realize that organic material plays a much bigger role in soil than just nutrient supply. Agriculturalists are now beginning to understand the partnership that soil bacteria and plants share. Recent agricultural studies have revealed the complexity of the soil's ecosystem and have shown that organic matter and bacteria introduced into the soil through composting drastically improve its structure, aeration and water retention. Soil organisms suppress diseases and release stored nutrients over time. Though organic material needs to be only a small percentage (3 to 5 percent) of the soil, the bacterial life that it supports and the nutrients that it brings to the plants are essential to soil fertility. Organic matter is not soluble in water, so it does not wash away in the rain. It also stores nutrients, which are slowly released by microorganisms into a form that plants can use. This storage of nutrients in the soil is much more beneficial than the water-soluble chemical fertilizers that seep unused from our gardens and farms into our waterways and ecosystems.

Traditional organic methods of agriculture are returning as people realize the mistake of relying too heavily on chemical fertilizers. The production of these chemicals involves manufacturing and mining processes that pollute and harm the environment. In contrast, composting and organic fertilizers help the environment by reducing our need for landfills.

More than ever before, people today are aware of the impact waste has on the environment. There is a growing urgency in Canadian culture to be environmentally conscientious of the consequences of consumption and waste. Composting provides an opportunity to responsibly deal with our waste in a positive way at little to no cost. The recognition of the value of all compost can do for us has resulted in a gradual shift back in the direction of organic gardening.

The Benefits of Composting

People have a special connection with the earth. Many gardeners describe feeling rather Zen-like as they dig into a soft pile of dirt. The sense of contentment and being part of nature is the driving force behind why many people get out and garden. That feeling is multiplied when you get actively involved in the composting process. Like a baker, you mix the right ingredients, stir it up, cook it (or rather, the bacteria cook it) and serve the results to an appreciative recipient—in this case a garden that will thank you and beam its approval throughout the growing season. Actively participating in composting gives you a sense of accomplishment because you become part of nature's process.

It's not difficult, either. Just pile it up, fluff it up and add water. That is the motto for a successful backyard compost pile.

Compost:

- Saves you money
- Provides a balanced diet of nutrients to your plants
- Stores and releases nutrients over time
- Retains water and aerates the soil
- Fights disease
- Prevents erosion
- Balances PH
- Reduces waste and helps the environment

Composting is an activity that is accessible to everyone. Schools, balcony gardeners and homeowners can all find space and use for a compost bin. For example, if you are the proud owner of a yard full of grass, a compost pile will deal with your grass clippings, and you can use the finished compost as top-dressing to reduce the need for watering, fertilizer and herbicides. If you are an apartment dweller with a respectable container garden on your balcony or just a few potted plants inside by the window, composting with an indoor worm bin will improve the health and growth of your houseplants and will protect them from soil-borne diseases, while providing free fishing bait!

Financial Savings

When you produce your own compost, you reduce your lawn and garden expenses. Compost is full of nutrients and organic matter, so by adding compost to your garden, you save money that would otherwise be spent purchasing soil conditioners and fertilizers. You can also save money on bagged wood chips by using compost as a mulch to suppress unwanted weeds. Compost helps plants fight disease and is a great natural alternative to purchasing pesticides and herbicides. Spreading compost on your lawn will make your grass so healthy that weeds won't have any room to grow. You can also reduce your water bill because compost helps retain moisture in your soil. Cut down on the cost of peat moss and potting soil by using fully cured compost instead.

All plants benefit from the addition of compost.

Balanced Diet of Nutrients for Your Plants

Compost is a soil amendment that is full of nutrients. It is not as potent as an organic fertilizer, but it does contain all the macronutrients (such as phosphorus, nitrogen and potassium) and micronutrients (such as copper, iron, zinc and nickel) that your plants need. When you send your grass clippings, yard waste and kitchen scraps out for garbage collection, you deprive your soil of the nutrients stored in those items. Nature's cycle is cut short, and the plants in your garden start to deplete the soil of nutrients. Throwing out the nutrients stored in your yard waste and then purchasing fertilizers makes no sense, especially when you consider that inorganic fertilizers often contain only macronutrients and lack the many micronutrients your plants need. Think of compost as a multivitamin that renews your soil. Compost works in combination with an organic fertilizer such as manure to provide a balanced diet for your soil. In time and after several applications, compost can sufficiently feed your plants, eliminating the need for fertilizer.

Controlled Nutrition Release

Compost is full of organic matter and microorganisms. Unlike chemical fertilizers, organic matter is not soluble in water and will not be washed away by rain or excessive watering. Locked away within that organic matter are all the nutrients your plants need to thrive.

Microorganisms in the soil break down the organic matter into smaller pieces called colloids, which provide nutrients your plants can absorb. The release of the nutrients to your plants is slow and is controlled by the rate of microbial growth. Amazingly, bacteria flourish in the soil during peak growing times, supplying the right amount of nutrients just when your plants need them.

In contrast, chemical fertilizers and pesticides may increase production for a time, but they often work against the complexities of the soil's ecosystem in the long run. The introduction of chemicals can kill many microorganisms and damage the rate of microbial activity. Unlike the slow release of nutrients provided by the organic ecosystem, chemical fertilizers need to be soluble in water to be usable by your plants and will drain away in the rain or with over-watering, so they require constant reapplication. As the chemical fertilizers drain from your soil, they pollute the water table below and eventually build up in our rivers and waterways. One advantage to choosing organic matter over chemical fertilizers is that the organic nutrients stay where you put them.

Improved Aeration and Water Retention

If you use inorganic fertilizers for a prolonged period, the quality of your soil will degrade over time. Use of chemical fertilizers kills decomposers in the soil and limits your garden's ability to renew organic matter. The soil will likely start to show signs of erosion and will have trouble with water retention.

Organic matter in soil greatly improves aeration and water retention.

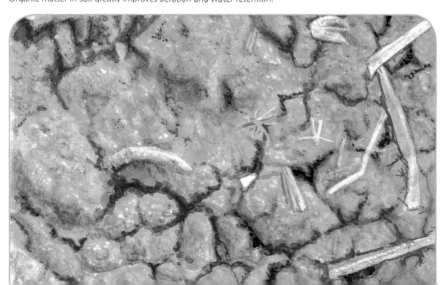

One simple solution to any soil structure problem is to add compost to your soil. The miracle and mystery of compost is that it is a binding agent for sandy soils, providing the glue that holds them together and helps them retain water, while also fixing clayey soils by adding air spaces and improving the soil's drainage (see Appendix B for more information about identifying soil types).

The organic matter in compost is of varying sizes and shapes. When mixed in with a clayey soil, the organic matter becomes coated with a thin film of water, but its irregular shape creates air pockets that allow bacteria and the plant roots to breathe.

When compost is mixed with sandy soil, the fungi, worms and organic matter in the compost produce binding agents that act as a gel to hold the soil particles together. This binding is called aggregate formation. Aggregated soil holds equal parts of air and water and is integral to the health of your soil and plants.

Disease Resistance

Your compost pile is a battleground for a succession of garden-variety bacteria vying for dominance and survival. Compost is full of beneficial super bacteria that have the stamina to kill many of the harmful viruses and bacteria that can attack your plants. Much like the T cells of the human immune system, the beneficial bacteria attack and kill any invading plant diseases.

Compost cannot cure an infected plant, but it can prevent future infection. Using compost reduces your need to purchase and use fungicides and pesticides.

These chemicals do not distinguish between good and bad bacteria and will decimate the beneficial bacteria populations in your soil, eliminating the immunity they provide and leaving your soil vulnerable to the next attack. The less chemicals you use, the better off your plants and soil will be.

Compost helps plants fight soil-borne diseases that can affect plant growth and health. Both of the above plants were introduced to a soil disease. The plant on the top was pre-treated with compost, whereas the plant on the bottom was not.

Erosion Reduction

Erosion is the gradual loss of topsoil that occurs when we leave our soil vulnerable to wind and rain. In nature, a plant's roots hold the soil in place, and its leaves and root network protect against wind, controlling erosion. Think of a prairie field full of grass or a forest full of trees; the soil stays put because an overhang of vegetation protects it. Exposed soil is vulnerable to erosion, which is a concern for farmers or people with large, open gardens.

Erosion from water often occurs when drops of rain bounce off the soil. The impact of the droplet causes little dents in the surface of the soil, which collect water and eventually develop into channels. As water flows through these channels, soil is picked up and carried away. Compost can protect your soil from water erosion. The sponge-like quality of compost absorbs the impact of the falling water droplets and expands to hold the water, keeping the soil and nutrients in place.

Compost protects against wind erosion by contributing to aggregate formation and by retaining water. The resulting soil is heavier and less likely to separate into dust particles small enough to be moved in the air.

Balanced Soil pH

A substance's level of acidity or alkalinity is expressed numerically as a pH value, where a pH of 1.0 is extremely acidic and a pH of 14 is extremely alkaline. Different species of plants are suited to varying levels of soil pH. Soil pH usually ranges between an acidic level of 6.0 and an alkaline level of 8.0. In high-alkaline soil, you may have trouble growing plants that do best in acidic conditions, such as blueberries, and in acidic soil, you may have trouble growing alkaline-loving plants, such as chicory. Even worse, what do you do if you want to grow a variety of plants that all require different ranges of pH? One easy solution is to add compost. Balanced feedstock composed of both acidic and alkaline ingredients will act as a buffer to allow plants to thrive regardless of soil pH. Plants thrive in a specific pH range because certain

Cover exposed soil in your garden with compost to reduce erosion.

Plants for Acidic Soil

Scientific Name	Common Name
Abies	Fir
Digitalis	Foxglove
Gaultheria	Wintergreen
Juniperus	Juniper
Picea	Spruce
Primula	Primrose
Quercus	Oak
Rhododendron	Azalea
Taxus	Yew
Vaccinium	Blueberry

Plants for Alkaline Soil

Scientific Name	Common Name
Acer	Maple
Celtis	Hackberry
Hemerocallis	Daylily
Hosta hybrids	Plantain Lily
Juniperus	Juniper
Monarda	Bee Balm
Populus	Poplar, Cottonwood
Robinia	Locusts
Salvia	Sage
Thymus	Thyme

Making a Purple Cabbage pH Indicator Test Kit

1. Cook 1 to 2 cups of purple cabbage in the microwave for 3 to 5 minutes (until soft).
2. Soak a white coffee filter in the cabbage juices.
3. Air dry the filter and cut it into strips.
4. Dip the cabbage paper strips into water-based acid or base solutions and look for colour

pH	2	4	6	8	10	12
Colour	Red	Purple	Violet	Blue	Blue-green	Greenish yellow

nutrients are only available or soluble in acidic or alkaline conditions. The release of nutrients from compost is not dependant on a pH level, which makes those nutrients available to the plants.

Test the pH of your soil by using litmus paper or a pH probe purchased from a garden centre, or by making your own purple cabbage pH indicator test kit.

Waste Reduction

One spring, summer or autumn day, take a walk through the alleys and streets of your neighbourhood on garbage day. You will likely see that at least a few people on every block have a stack of bags full of grass, leaves and other yard waste. It boggles the mind to think that all the nutrients stored in that waste will end up locked away in a landfill instead of being returned to the soil.

A landfill is not a place where you want waste to break down. When all that good organic matter starts to decompose, it creates leachate and methane—toxic substances that your municipality spends

millions of dollars to keep out of the environment and the air.

As the populations of our cities increase, and landfill space gets more and more sparse, communities are searching for alternatives ways to deal with their waste. The first step many cities took was to introduce recycling programs. They now collect plastics, paper, glass and metal and sell it back to industry as a resource for manufacturing new materials. Pop bottles turn into polar fleece, newspapers are transformed into roof shingles and glass pickle jars end up in the reflective paint used on road signs. Until recently, none of the industries wanted to try to convert organic matter into a new product, and the value of large-scale municipal composting was ignored.

Today, many communities consider composting a viable alternative to using landfills. After battling controversy for sending barges of garbage to the U.S., Toronto began a composting program in 2002 and has been using it to divert almost one-third of its waste from the

Many towns and cities use a windrow compost system.

landfill. Many communities are resorting to alternate means of waste disposal as their landfills run out of room. Some communities burn their garbage, creating smog and pollution; others dump it in the ocean so it can wash up on their neighbours' shores. Some have even considered shooting garbage into space. Composting is a good alternative to relying solely on landfills because it deals with the garbage on location in a safe, non-polluting way without affecting neighbouring communities. Indeed, many communities appreciate the opportunity to buy the resulting compost.

You may have been told by your municipality to start separating your "green" waste; your kitchen scraps, yard waste and even bathroom tissue go into a special green bin for the waste collector. Most towns and cities collecting green waste

use a windrow compost system. Enormous, steaming rows of organic waste are churned up and moved around by front-end loaders and special digging machinery. The end result is screened and used for erosion control, land

Bird's eye view of Edmonton's Waste Management Centre

Woodchips absorb and clean smelly air outside the facility.

reclamation projects, cleaning petroleum-contaminated soil, agricultural projects and more.

A great example of large-scale composting can be found in Edmonton. To most people, Edmonton is known for the largest centre of consumption in the country, West Edmonton Mall; however,

few people know that Edmonton also hosts the world's largest indoor composter. The stainless steel aeration building is the size of four CFL football fields. It takes only 28 days for garbage to go in one end of the composter and come out the other end as compost. Dignitaries from around the world have come to see this wonder of composting wonders in hopes of taking home a few ideas. In the administration building at the Waste Management Centre, a world map covered with pins shows the many countries from which people have travelled to see the facility. Mongolia, Australia and Brazil are just a few of the countries marked on the map.

What makes this composting mecca so special? Well, it is one of the few facilities that takes in mixed residential solid and sewage waste. The people of Edmonton are privileged in that they

Beltline of waste inside the composting facility

do not have to sort their garbage into special green waste bins. Instead, the city just loads all the garbage into one end of the composter, mixes it with the treated biosolids from the sewage plant and screens out anything that doesn't have the good graces to decompose after a month of intense composting. This way, Edmonton doesn't miss any composting opportunities. From brown meat paper to used diapers, all the organic material is diverted—cutting the city's waste footprint in half. Of the 240,000 tonnes of garbage Edmonton produces every year, 120,000 tonnes of it are composted, resulting in 50,000 tonnes of compost that is sold to industries in need of good soil.

Edmonton is Canada's leading city in waste reduction, not because the people are particularly passionate about waste (though many of them really are)

These zinnias have benefited from the addition of compost.

but because they had no choice but to change their habits. In 1988, the city's last landfill was nearing its capacity, and the waste department started looking around for a new location. Local residents and environmental groups shot down every site that was proposed for a new landfill. Like most people, Edmontonians wanted to dispose of their waste but not in a place where they could see it. The "not in my backyard" mentality was evident no matter where the city proposed to go. As a result, city officials had to see how much longer they could stretch out the lifespan of the existing landfill. They started one of Canada's earliest curbside recycling programs and cut out 18 percent of the city's waste, experimenting with all different kinds of commercial composting pilots before deciding to build the Edmonton Composting Facility. This year, after stretching the Clover Bar Landfill 20 years past its expected expiry date, the city's landfill will finally close. With the combined efforts of composting, recycling and a new gasification system that will start up in 2010, Edmonton will be diverting more than 90 percent of its waste away from the landfill.

But even if you live in a city like Edmonton that has mastered the art of commercial composting, it doesn't mean home composting is defunct or unnecessary. Home composting is still an important part of reducing our ecological footprint. Much focus has been placed on global warming and how we can reduce our carbon emissions. Logically, when you compost at home, you produce less waste for the collectors. Their trucks don't fill up as fast, and they make fewer trips, reducing how much they drive. As well, you save tax dollars because the city does not have to pay for the disposal—landfills and commercial composting are expensive. Home composting is especially important during peak disposal seasons like spring and autumn yard cleanup time, when yard waste floods the waste collection system and cannot all be processed by even the largest composter, meaning that the overflow may end up in the landfill. If everybody took the opportunity to compost at home, so much energy and time would be saved.

My whole life has been spent waiting for an epiphany, a manifestation of God's presence, the kind of transcendent, magical experience that lets you see your place in the big picture. And that is what I had with my first compost heap.

–Bette Midler

Getting Started

Choosing the Right Method

If you are reading this book, you've probably already made the decision to start composting. The big question is, how do you get started? The first thing is to choose the best composting method for you. There are four major categories of composting: aeration (aerobic), on-site, anaerobic and vermicomposting (composting with worms). The first three are typically outdoor compost systems that require some sort of yard or garden to work in; the fourth system can be either indoor or outdoor depending on the climate in which you live.

Choosing the method of composting you want depends on a few factors. You must consider how much effort you want to put into getting finished compost, how quickly you want to produce it, what types and volume of material you want to process, how much of the finished product you can use and, most importantly, how tolerant your family and neighbours are. Each type of composting is introduced in the following pages. Once you have decided which type you would like to try, turn to the section in the book that more thoroughly describes how to do it.

Choosing the Right Method for You

Compost Method	Pros	Cons	Typical User
Aeration composting	• is fast • processes high volumes of waste • suitable for most kitchen and yard waste • has no odour • can be low to no cost • produces usable finished product	• requires work • may have to buy or construct bin • pest management can be an issue	• is an active gardener • has a yard or garden that produces large volumes of yard waste (grass clippings, weeds, annuals, autumn leaves)
On-site composting	• requires little effort • blends in with surroundings • suppresses weeds	• is slow • not suitable for kitchen scraps • produces no usable end product	• has flower or ornamental gardens • needs mulch around the base of shrubbery or in an unused corner of a vegetable garden
Anaerobic composting	• reduces waste • can process all kitchen waste • requires little effort • few pest problems	• is slow • can smell foul • requires an airtight container (may have cost)	• mid-sized family interested in waste reduction • has a small, low maintenance yard • is not an active gardener
Worm composting	• is fast and easy • requires little space • results in a rich finished product • reduces waste • works throughout winter • is a good educational tool for children	• can be difficlut to convince squeamish family members • suffers occasional fruit fly problems • requires monitoring • can have start-up cost (buying worms and bin) • not suitable for yard waste	• small family with young children • singles, couples with small or no yard • winter composters • people with house plants

Aeration Composting

When most people think of composting, an image of a pile of mixed yard waste and kitchen scraps topped with a smattering of eggshells may come to mind. You might have seen a fancy black bin with a little sliding door at the bottom or an enormous three-bin wooden structure full of grass clippings and leaves. This pile-it-up-in-the-open method is called aeration composting and is the most common method used by gardeners and commercial composting professionals.

"Aeration composting" simply means composting that allows air to access the pile. This method is and always has been the most popular method of composting because it yields the fastest results, has no foul smell and can produce high volumes of compost. The bacteria that work the hardest and reproduce the quickest require an aerobic compost pile because, like most organisms, they need air to breathe. Aeration composting often (but not always) involves the active participation of the gardener to get the job done. Depending on how you build your compost pile, you may have to dig into the pile to mix it around every once in a while and add some water on occasion to make sure the microorganisms in the pile are happy and are doing what they should. Aeration composting can be done in one big batch that you mix up all at once and wait until it is finished before using, or you can add to the pile throughout the season and remove finished compost as you go. A successful aerobic pile heats up to kill weed seeds and produce compost quickly, though not all piles need to heat up to produce compost.

Aeration composting is the most common method.

Aerobic compost piles can be in a bin, in a rotating barrel or out in the open. The climate and local pest population will determine if and what kind of encasement you might need for your pile.

If you are interested in trying aeration composting, turn to page 33 to get started.

On-site Composting

If you want to improve the quality of the soil in a particular location and want to plant in the compost pile right away, try on-site composting. On-site composters are not big, obvious piles; rather, they blend with the environment, spread out like a forest floor. Usually built over problem areas, on-site composters suppress the growth of weeds where they are situated and provide a healthy space for your plants to grow. These composters are meant to handle yard waste such as grass and leaves; do not add kitchen scraps to on-site composters. The pile does not need to be turned or aerated because it is usually too shallow to become compacted. It also does not heat up. Instead, the larger macroorganisms, such as worms and beetles, do most of the work breaking it down.

If you are interested in trying on-site composting, turn to page 85 to get started.

Anaerobic Composting

Arguably the least popular method of composting, anaerobic composting involves depriving your compost pile of air. Microorganisms that can survive without air will break down the content of your compost pile. It takes longer

Using straw mulch is a form of on-site composting.

than aerobic composting and has the unfortunate by-product of sometimes letting off putrid gas. Most people who have an anaerobic pile started with an aerobic one, got a bit distracted and didn't notice that the biology of the pile had changed until they started getting complaints from the neighbours about the smell.

However, anaerobic composting is not always an accident. Some people choose anaerobic composting because it requires little effort and is great for waste reduction. And, when done right, nasty smells will not scare friends and family away. Typically done underground, anaerobic composting can be as simple as digging a hole, filling it up with kitchen waste, covering it over and returning a year later for the finished product. You can also purchase special airtight containers, or make your own airtight bin using a lidded garbage can or 20 L pail. Anaerobic piles do not heat up and are often meant for batch composting, meaning that once you have collected enough scraps to make the pile of raw material, you seal it up and don't add any new material. Unlike worm and aerobic composting, certain anaerobic systems do allow you to compost meat, bones and milk products, but the end product has restricted uses.

If you are interested in trying anaerobic composting, turn to page 93 to get started. turn to page 93

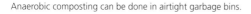

Anaerobic composting can be done in airtight garbage bins.

Worm composting is ideal for people with limited space.

Worm Composting

Also known as vermicomposting, keeping a bin full of worms to break down your kitchen scraps is an increasingly popular method of producing compost. The most common reason for choosing to have a worm compost bin is waste reduction. Usually an energetic person in charge of a commercial kitchen, restaurant or school cafeteria will set up a big bin full of worms just outside the delivery door. Some apartment dwellers also choose to have a compost bin indoors. Worm bins thrive on kitchen scraps and do not typically process yard waste in large volume unless it is used as bedding when starting the bin. Therefore, people who don't have access to a big yard can still benefit from the opportunity to reduce waste while creating rich compost for their houseplants.

Finished vermicompost is great for regular gardeners as well. It is different from backyard compost in that it is more than just a soil conditioner; it is classified as a fertilizer, too. A little bit goes a long way and does a lot to improve the fertility of your garden soil. Keep in mind, however, that most worm bins need to be kept indoors over the winter, and squeamish family members may need some convincing to allow your new wormy pets a place in your home.

To find out more about worm composting, turn to page 106 to get started.

Composting Tools

Once you have decided which composting method you think you'd like to try, you may want to visit your local hardware store for some tools. Composting requires few specialty tools, most of which are usually already present in most gardeners' sheds.

Compost Aerator

Any stick or dowel with a pointy end that you can poke into a compost pile works as well as an aerator. However, there are several fancy models that you can purchase from a garden centre or hardware store. One type has wings that fold out when you pull the aerator out of the pile. The wings can be twisted about to get maximum fluffing action as the aerator is pulled out of the pile. Another high-end model is called a "compost crank"; this model screws in a circular motion deep into the pile, and you pull the crank upward to mix around the contents.

If you purchase the style of aerator that you have to plunge into the composter, make sure it has a sharp, pointy end so it can cut through to at least the middle of the pile. You'll also need a bit of energy and an elevated position to really stab it in there. If you choose to use an aerator instead of turning the pile the old fashioned way, use it regularly so the pile stays light and fluffy. Once the pile is compacted, it will be very difficult to penetrate with the aerator.

Composting tools are often no different from gardening tools.

Some people have reported that using a 3" (7.5 cm) bulb auger attached to a cordless drill is an easy way to mix up the pile.

Compost or Garden Fork

Many composting enthusiasts swear by their compost forks for aerating a compost pile. The long, round tines are widespread so the compost ingredients won't get stuck on them. The round shape lets the fork slide into the pile easily to turn its contents.

If you plan to use your fork to add compost to your soil, consider buying a digging fork instead. The tines are thicker and shorter and are designed to break up tough, compacted soil. The digging fork is shorter but is often heavier because it is built so that it won't bend under pressure.

A solid fork constructed of a single piece of metal is your best option. At the very least, the fork you choose should have a head made of sturdy steel so it is durable and does not warp or bend under pressure.

Compost Screen

You can purchase a screen or make it yourself. Either way, a screen with holes 6 to 12 mm wide is best if you plan to use compost in a potting mix or as a top-dressing. You don't need a screen if you plan on digging the compost directly into the soil.

The screen's edges should be at least 5 cm high so the compost stays inside as you shuffle it over the screen. The larger the surface of the screen, the more

compost you can process at once. However, don't make it too big because you'll need to lift and move it over to your compost pile.

Compost Thermometer

You need a compost thermometer only if you are serious about hot aeration composting. The thermometer is plunged into the centre of the pile and left there. Every day, you can check the pile's internal temperature. If you pay attention to the readings, you'll see the compost heat up after a few days and then start to cool again, which indicates the pile is ready to be turned. If you don't plan on hot composting your pile, don't bother purchasing the compost thermometer.

Compost thermometer

Gloves

Always wear gloves in the garden and while composting to protect your hands from sharp twigs, wet wastes, dirt and bugs. Most decomposers are safe to handle with your bare hands; however, some have the potential to make you seriously ill. Though uncommon, you can contract tetanus, paronychia (also known as nail biter's nightmare) and several respiratory diseases, including Legionnaires' disease, from handling soil or compost without gloves or with wet gloves. Keep several pairs of gardening gloves handy so you always have a dry pair on hand in case the ones you are wearing get wet. Use rubber gloves while watering or when digging your hands into wet wastes. Always keep your tetanus shots up to date just in case.

Hose, Rain Barrel or Watering Can

As you build your pile, add water to any dry materials. A rain barrel is a great source of non-chlorinated water that will not hurt the decomposers in your pile. Alternatively, you can let tap water sit in a large watering can overnight so the chlorine evaporates, and use that water on your pile instead. If you don't want to dechlorinate, that's okay, too; most of the decomposers will survive. Use a hose with a wide spray nozzle so the dry feedstock will be evenly coated with water.

Kitchen Catcher

If you plan to compost kitchen wastes, you will need a kitchen catcher. A kitchen catcher is a fancy name for a pail or bucket in which you temporarily store your kitchen wastes before bringing them out to the compost pile. Empty your kitchen catcher into your garden at least once a week (every couple of days is best). Find a bucket that is large enough to suit your family's needs.

A kitchen catcher without a lid or with air holes lets air into the pile and keeps smells down but is vulnerable to flies. A kitchen catcher with a lid keeps flies out but may smell bad and turn anaerobic.

Rain barrel

Keep flies and smells away by using a small container, about the size of a yogourt or margarine tub, to store wastes in the fridge and empty it daily into a larger bucket with a lid that you keep just outside your back door. Empty the larger tub into the composter once a week.

Alternatively, purchase a commercial model kitchen catcher with a carbon filter on the lid to keep down smells and prevent flies from getting in the bin. Rinse any kitchen catcher after you empty it to keep the bin from getting overly smelly.

Machete or Hand Axe

One fast, fun way to chop up yard and kitchen wastes is to use a machete or hand axe. Be careful that small children are not in the vicinity, and keep all hands away from the blade while it's in use. A machete or axe should always be used with a chopping block; use a piece of scrap plywood on a stand or a good-sized tree stump. Sharpen the machete with a whetstone after every use. Sharpen a hand axe with a metal file.

Metal Files and Whetstones

Do you want a shovel that can easily dig into compact soil? Do you want a lawn mower that preserves the health of your grass? The easiest way to make sure your tools are working to their greatest potential is to keep their blades sharp. Use a steel file (known as a mill bastard file) or whetstone to sharpen your tools after each use.

Not sure how to use a file? Sit down and get a firm grip on the tool with the blade pointing away from you. Set the file on the edge of the blade at approximately a 20-degree angle. Push the file so it slides along the blade while maintaining the same angle. Continue filing the whole length of the blade. If you want an extra sharp edge, flip the blade over and file the other side, too.

Mulching Lawn Mower

Most people with a lawn already own a mower. If you need to buy one, consider purchasing a mulching model. You can use it to grasscycle or to chop materials for your compost pile.

Pruning Shears and Scissors

Also known as hand pruners or secateurs, pruning shears are heavy-duty scissors that can cut and clip almost any bit of yard waste. Use them to cut up material before you put it in your compost pile.

Twigs, corncobs and long annual stems should be chopped up so they will break down quickly. Choose a set of shears that fits comfortably in your hand. Some of the more expensive models have a crank system that allows you to cut through thick branches even if you don't have the hand strength of an orangutan.

For food wastes and easily cut yard wastes, use an old, cheap pair of scissors to save your pruning shears from becoming dull unnecessarily.

Rakes

In autumn, it is always handy to have a broad, fan-shaped, plastic, bamboo or aluminum leaf rake to gather up leaves. In spring, you can use a leaf rake to clean up or remove old mulches that need to be replaced and to spread new mulches around your plants. In summer, a rake is useful for breaking up clumps of grass on your lawn so they decompose easier.

Garden rakes can be used to spread dirt or compost on the garden's surface or to spread around heavy inorganic mulches like gravel or rocks.

Shovels

A shovel is a useful tool for a variety of garden projects. In composting, a shovel is best used for digging into the garden to apply finished compost and for moving the compost to a new location.

Shovels come in many different shapes and sizes, so you may want to purchase a few different models for the various jobs you have to do around the bin.

A shovel with a pointed blade is best for digging. A short shovel with a square end and handled with a D-grip is good for chopping rough yard waste before putting it in your bin. A short shovel with a narrow head and a handle is great for accessing compost from commercial units that have little doors at the bottom.

The most important things to watch for when purchasing a shovel are that it fits comfortably in your hands, that it is not too heavy to work with, and that it is good quality. Nothing is worse than a cheap model with a head that falls off, a shaft that splits or a handle that wiggles. Pay the couple of extra bucks for a solidly constructed shovel and save yourself some frustration. Even better, look for a completely metal shovel that has the blade, shaft and handle welded into one solid piece.

A garden fork, rake and shovel are all useful composting tools.

Shredder

Gardeners with a large yard that has many prunings and annuals to clean up in autumn or spring will find a shredder very useful. The shredder makes short work of your trimmings so they break down quickly in the compost pile. If you have only a small garden, consider teaming up with neighbours to rent a unit from a local hardware store or garden centre.

Storage Containers and Buckets

Buckets are useful for moving, storing and mixing all sorts of garden wastes. If you plan to store wastes for later use in a compost pile, consider purchasing big bins with lids to protect the wastes from the rain. Put them beside the composter for easy access. Storage bins look tidier than garbage bags and are less fragile.

When storing dry wastes, such as autumn leaves, drill holes into sides of the bin to make sure the pile gets air. For wet kitchen wastes, layer sawdust every few centimetres so the pile doesn't turn anaerobic. Don't store kitchen wastes for more than three weeks, and rinse the container between uses.

Containers are also handy for storing finished compost, small tools and garden supplies, as well as for making potting soil mixes with your finished compost.

Tarps

A good plastic tarp is great for covering finished compost, protecting open piles on rainy or sunny days, dragging piles of waste around the yard, solar heating a patch of soil and suffocating the weeds in a certain area. You may want to buy a few, depending on your needs. Purchase a tarp that is large enough to serve its purpose and that has grommets along its edges to easily stake or tie the tarp in place. Don't buy a tarp that is too big; it will be a hassle to move around and keep tidy.

Maintaining Your Tools

The best way to get the most out of your tools is to treat and store them properly. After you are finished using them, clean off any dirt, mud or debris. Leave them to dry in the sun before you put them away. Wooden shafts and handles start to break down or rot if they are put away wet. Sharpen the blades of your shovels, axes and other metal tools. Prevent your tools from rusting by rubbing them with an oily rag to form a thin coat of oil. Store your tools in a shed or garage where they will be protected. Never leave your tools sitting outside on the ground where they can get wet and damaged. Plan for a 10 to 20 minute cleanup session after digging around in the garden or compost pile.

However small your garden, you must provide for two of the serious gardener's necessities—a tool shed and a compost heap.

–Anne Scott-James

Basics of Great Backyard Aeration Composting

If, like many Canadians, you are happy to get down and dirty with soil, you may be thinking of giving aeration composting a try. The key to successful aeration composting is to create an environment in which the decomposers will thrive. If the decomposers are happy, they will quickly reproduce and break down your wastes.

How Aeration Composting Works

Most decomposition in an aeration compost pile is done by microorganisms: bacteria (especially actinomycetes) protozoa and fungi. Bacteria do the bulk of the work. There are many different kinds of bacteria in your pile. Mesophiles are bacteria that live at room temperature and thrive in temperatures slightly higher (10° to 45° C). Yogourt, beer, wine and cheese cultures are mesophiles. *E. coli* and tetanus cultures are also mesophiles, which is why you should keep your tetanus shots current and always wear gloves while gardening.

Mesophiles breathe in oxygen and work at breaking down easily digestible feedstocks such as starches and carbohydrates. They are fairly simple creatures that emit enzymes to break down their foods. As they metabolize these foods, they produce what you could call body heat. Several chemical processes occur, including oxidation and hydrolysis (splitting water into new compounds). After about two days, the temperature rises to a level high enough for a new generation of bacteria to flourish.

Thermophiles lay dormant in a pile until it reaches 40° C. Once the thermophiles get going, they heat the pile up to temperatures too high for the mesophiles to live (50° to 70° C). Thermophiles are faster decomposers and can break down some of the harder cellulose fibres, fats and proteins. Once the thermophiles have done their job and eaten all the readily available food, the pile temperature drops. Fungi and actinomycetes cure the pile and break down lignin from woody wastes and other hardy feedstocks. Some of the mesophiles then return to the pile. The bodies of the dead thermophiles and mesophiles contribute to the humus of the pile.

Throughout this process, the compost pile usually hosts other larger organisms that help break down the larger wastes, making them available to the microorganisms. These larger organisms include worms, mites, beetles, sow bugs and springtails, to name a few. When the pile heats up, these critters move to the cooler edges of the pile, returning to the middle when it cools down again.

The decomposers will do their work as long as the pile contains everything they need to survive and flourish. They need air to breathe, moisture to aid in the chemical processes of digestion and reproduction and the right balance of food to promote reproduction and growth.

Getting Started with Aeration Composting

Most gardeners have experimented with aeration composting at some point in time and have found that not every pile behaves the same way. Composting is not a perfect science, and it involves a bit of trial and error. You first need to choose an appropriate aeration method and bin to suit your needs and then build the contents of the bin, keeping in mind the four basic elements of a healthy compost pile: good location, air, water and the correct feedstock. If you provide your pile with each of these elements, it will be a success.

Given the right conditions, aeration methods quickly produce usable compost.

Adding Air: Hot and Cold Composting Methods

It is no coincidence that aeration composting is pronounced "air-ation" composting. Air is vital to the success of the compost pile. The quickest and best decomposers need air to breathe. Without air they will die, and a new group of anaerobic composters will take over and stink up your pile.

Before you start composting, you must decide how you plan to get air into your pile. This decision will affect the style of bin you choose and how you care for your pile. There are two basic methods of aeration: active turning and passive planning. Active turning is for hot composting, and passive planning is for cold composting. The method you choose should be determined by the speed at which you want to produce compost, the intensity of effort you are willing to put in and the supply of feedstock available to you.

Traditional compost professionals suggest hot composting is the best and most efficient way to compost. However, cold composting is gaining popularity with many backyard gardeners who don't want to bother turning their piles or who don't have the volume of waste required for hot composting. The following table describes the advantages and disadvantages of each method.

Hot vs. Cold Composting

Compost Method	Pros	Cons
Hot composting (active turning aeration)	• is fast • can kill pathogens and weed seeds • wards off pests (mice, wasps, flies, etc.) • processes large volumes of waste	• is labour intensive • is a batch system • kills off some disease-fighting microorganisms • oxidation causes nitrogen loss
Cold composting (passive planning aeration)	• is easy, requiring little labour • can add wastes constantly • retains nitrogen • has many beneficial microorganisms	• can turn anaerobic • can attract pests • does not kill pathogens or weed seeds • is slow

A good compost pile should get hot enough to poach an egg, but not so hot it would cook a lobster.

–Anonymous

Hot Active Turning Methods

If your garden produces a large amount of waste during spring or autumn cleanup, you may want to consider hot composting the wastes so you can produce compost in time for the next growing season. Hot composting happens when an appropriate mix of feedstock and water are available in a large enough pile and are mixed regularly. The pile usually needs to be about 1.2 m³ in size to insulate the hot core of the pile. Build the batch to the appropriate size right away using available wastes. Once the pile is built, do not add new wastes; instead, set them aside for your next batch.

Turning your pile fluffs it up and allows air to get in, therefore ensuring that you have aerobic decomposers throughout. Turning also gives you an opportunity to break up any clumps of anaerobic wastes to get air into those spaces for faster decomposition.

Turning and mixing the pile changes its bioavailability. The first set of decomposers in the middle of your pile heat it up as they consume the available feedstock. When they start to run out of food, the pile starts to cool. If you turn the pile at this point, the decomposers have access to the undigested feedstock from the outside edges; the pile will heat up again, even hotter than before. Use a compost thermometer to monitor the heat. Typically, the pile will get really hot in about two days. The third or fourth day will see the pile start to cool, at which point you should turn it. If you continue to monitor the heat and turn the pile every time it starts to cool, you can have finished compost within three weeks.

A mass planting produces a large amount of waste at the end of the season that is best added to a hot compost pile.

If you choose not to use a compost thermometer, turn the pile after four days, then again once every 7 to 10 days afterward. You do not want to turn it too often because the decomposers require the insulation of the outer edges of the pile to keep warm. When you turn the pile, it loses heat.

If you don't turn the pile, it will cool off, and the weight of its contents will slowly compact over time, pushing out the air. Once the air is gone, the bacteria will die and new anaerobic bacteria will take over. Overwatering can also result in a loss of air spaces. Turning the pile brings water to the surface and gives it a chance to evaporate while also reintroducing air to the pile.

There are several ways to turn your pile effectively. You can dig into it with a shovel or compost fork to mix the pile in place. This method is very labour intensive, and it may be to difficult mix the whole pile. Another option is to transfer the pile to a new location (usually just beside the old one), making sure the outside edges of the pile end up on the inside of the new pile. Or, set up your pile in a rotating barrel compost bin, which makes turning the pile easy.

Though intensive aeration techniques take more energy and involvement than other methods, you get a finished product quickly and you have a better understanding of how your pile is progressing. Dig around in the pile once a week, keeping an eye out for symptoms of developing problems, which you can remedy before they get troublesome. Pests tend to stay away from an aerated

pile because it is too hot, disturbed too often and too active for them to want to set up a home.

Requirements of Successful Hot Composting:

- A pile at least 1 m x 1 m x 1 m in size
- A mixed batch of appropriate feedstock
- Monitoring moisture levels (damp not soggy)
- Turning the pile every 7 to 10 days

Cold Passive Planning Methods

If you don't mind waiting for your finished product, try passive aeration. With passive aeration, you can still make sure your pile has plenty of air, even if you don't plan on digging in the dirt very often. However, you need to put some thought into how to build your pile and how to structure it around aeration.

Cold composting takes longer than hot composting because the pile does not heat up after its initial rise in temperature. The decomposers eat what is available to them in the middle of the pile and then reduce in numbers. The remaining decomposers gradually turn to the feedstock on the outside edges, consuming most of it by the end of a season.

Most passive aeration bins are either ever-producing or batch systems. An ever-producing pile is one in which you continually add new feedstock to the top and remove finished compost from the bottom.

You don't need to turn an ever-producing compost pile—the undigested wastes at the top should be kept separate from the curing compost at the bottom. The stuff at the top is at a different decomposition stage with different decomposers doing the work, and turning would only disrupt that process.

The cold composter can be a batch system if you build the pile all at once and stop adding fresh waste to allow the pile to decompose evenly. With this batch system, you may want to turn the pile once midway through the season to inspect its progress and to move the undigested wastes from the outside to the inside of the pile for even composting. When the compost is finished at the end of the season, you can remove it from the bin and rebuild it with stored wastes.

A cold compost pile is typically smaller in volume than a hot compost pile and therefore is less prone to the settling and compaction that causes anaerobic conditions. However, you still need to plan for some sort of aeration to make sure the pile does not turn anaerobic.

Sticks and Twigs Method

Keeping air in your pile can be as easy as layering sticks and twigs throughout your compost pile. Sticks decompose slowly, and they'll hold the structure of your pile, preventing compression and maintaining the air spaces. Once the compost is finished, screen out the partly decomposed sticks, chop them into little pieces and put them in a new pile using fresh sticks and twigs to provide structure and aeration. This passive method of composting heats up at first, but it will cool down after a week and won't finish composting until at least one growing season has passed. If you start the pile in spring, you can expect finished compost come harvest time in autumn. You may want to turn your compost pile once or twice over the course of the year to ensure even decomposition of the contents. If you layer dowels into the pile, leave the ends poking out the side so you can shake them about every once in a while to fluff up the pile.

Elevated Air Currents Method

Try building your pile on a bed of gravel, loose rocks or straw, or on a wood pallet that is elevated by about 30 cm. As the pile heats up, warm air and carbon dioxide from the working organisms rise out of its top. This upward air movement forms a convex current, pulling cool air up through the bottom of the pile—but only if the bottom of the pile is exposed to air. This method works best in combination with the piping method described next.

Be warned that the aeration from this method is not perfect because the air forms channels as it moves through the pile, leaving some areas without air while other areas have too much and tend to dry out. You can solve this problem by poking a compost aerator device into the pile every week or so to create new channels. A dowel, such as a broken hockey stick, works well, as does a commercial aerator device from a local garden centre.

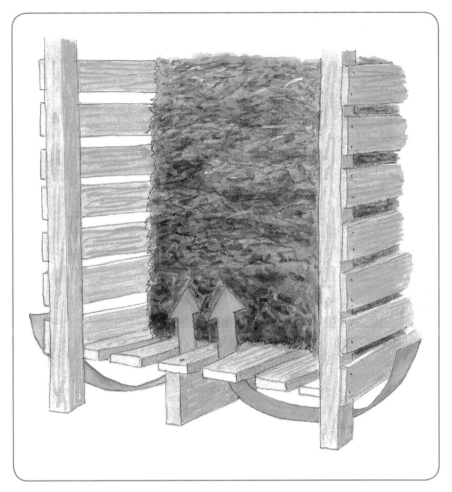

Elevated air currents method

Alternatively, layer in coarse brown materials, such as straw, whole autumn leaves and crumpled paper or cardboard, to make sure air pockets and voids are maintained throughout the pile despite how air circulates around it.

Piping Method

Build your pile on an elevated bed of straw or gravel. Buy a 1 to 1.2 m length of weeping tile or PVC 2" piping that has holes drilled into it every few centimetres. Bury one end of the pipe into the bedding and build your compost pile around the pipe so that it runs vertically through the length of your pile from top to bottom. The pipe will draw cool air from the bottom of the pile up through the centre. The holes will allow air to access the pile and will also make watering to the centre of the pile easier. Get creative and make homemade ventilation pipes if you don't want to venture out to buy piping. Loosely tie together a bundle of sticks or sunflower stalks and place them in the middle of your pile as you would the piping. You can also experiment with layers of horizontal piping at the bottom and centre of the compost pile. You will need several pipes layered throughout the pile. Wiggle the ends around from time to time to change the airflow and fluff up the pile.

To completely compost the pile, you may have to turn and rebuild it once or twice to make sure the materials on the outer edges completely decompose. You can get finished compost within one season. Soak the pipes in water to clean out any plugged air holes, and reuse the pipes in your next pile.

Aerator Method

If you make a nice compost pile in a bin that is too tall or narrow to really mix around the contents, you can purchase an aerator at your local garden centre. Various models of aerators are available, but you can also use any 1 m long dowel, such as an old broom handle or broken hockey stick. Jab the aerator deep into the pile, wiggle it about, pull it out and repeat until you are satisfied the pile is aerated. You can rotate the aerator around as you pull it out, so that the compost fluffs up. Poke your pile with the aerator at least once a month—every week is best. As long as you use the aerator consistently, you won't need to turn the pile more than once per season, if at all. You can expect finished compost within three to six months.

Piping method

Choose the right bin to suit your needs.

Choosing the Right Bin

Once you have decided which aeration method to use, you can select an appropriate bin to house the pile. Choosing the best type of bin or aerobic system depends on your needs and how much work you are willing to put in. Certain bins are more conducive to certain composting aeration methods than others; some make turning a hot pile easy while others are designed for cold composting. When choosing a bin, keep in mind how it will protect the compost pile against environmental conditions and local pest populations.

Your decision can also be based on aesthetics. You may have noticed your neighbour Sally's big, three-bin unit and thought, "Hey, she sure looks like a hard-core gardener with that big hulk in the yard. Maybe I should get one too." Alternatively, you may just have won a free compost bin from a draw, and now you need to know how to use it. You may want some compost right away, but you have a bad back and can't do too much heavy lifting. Whatever the case, there is an aeration compost unit that is right for you.

There are three major categories of aeration composting units: the single-bin unit, the three-bin unit and the rotating batch unit. The materials you use to build each unit can vary depending on your needs and available building supplies.

Single-bin Unit

The most popular method of backyard composting involves having one bin or an open pile to throw your kitchen scraps and yard waste in throughout the year. Single composting units are the choice of many people because they can be unobtrusive in size and blend in with the landscape. They are versatile in that you can do either cold or hot composting. Best of all, there is a large variety of units for sale and models that you can build to suit the look of your yard, prevent problem pests in your area and suit the environmental conditions you live with.

You can get compost quickly from the single-bin method if you get in and mix the pile around every week. However, some manufactured units have limited space, which makes turning the pile difficult and mixing the bottom of the pile with your shovel or compost fork near impossible if you keep the pile in place. If you don't structure the pile for aeration, and if you don't mix it, the pile will settle and close off the air spaces. It can become anaerobic and foul smelling if left unattended for too long.

Single-bin compost units are available commercially from garden centres and home building suppliers. You can also build one from old pallets, cement cinder blocks or whatever fits your fancy. The single bin needs to be at least 1.2 m³ to get hot and produce compost quickly. Keep in mind that many of the commercial compost units available are not large enough to provide the insulation necessary for hot composting. The manufacturers partly compensate for this by using black plastic casing that absorbs and transmits heat from the sun to your pile. However, you may find that the tall, narrow nature of the bin limits your ability to mix and aerate the compost. As you build your pile, you must consider how you plan to aerate it (see the Cold Passive Planning Methods section, p. 37).

Cool composting in a single bin allows you to throw your kitchen scraps in the top and scoop out finished compost from the bottom, though you'll have to wait longer for the finished result. If you structure your pile so that it has access to air, you will not need to do a lot of turning or mixing. This method also does not require that you save up materials for a batch; simply add materials as you produce them. The first items that you throw in will be ready first and can be scooped out from the bottom of the pile, and any matter that has not decomposed can be screened out and returned to the top of the pile.

Single-bin Compost Units

✓ Can be open-pile or closed-bin units

✓ Can be built to protect against any pests

✓ Can use hot or cold composting methods

✓ Can produce batch or ever-producing compost

✓ Are available in commercial models

✗ Can be difficult to turn

✓ Can use alternative aeration methods

Features to consider when purchasing or constructing a single-bin compost unit

Bin Features	Advantages	Disadvantages
Lid	• keeps pests out • prevents evaporation of water • reduces smells • has a pleasing appearance	• decreases aeration • reduces hot air currents in elevated piles
No lid	• easy to add new feed-stock • easy to poke with aeration device	• has no environmental control (evaporation and rain) • allows small pests access to the pile (flies, wasps)
Enclosed (4 walls) with no holes for aeration	• denies pests side access to the pile • pleasing appearance	• decreases aeration • difficult to turn or aerate
Enclosed (4 walls) with holes for aeration	• denies large pests side access to the pile • pleasing appearance • increases aeration	• allows small pests (ants, flies) access to the pile
Open pile (no bin)	• easy to turn • easy to build • suited to hot composting	• no environmental control (evaporation and rain) • no pest control • untidy appearance
Open front	• easy to turn	• no pest control • can have untidy appearance
Door (hinged or removable)	• easy to turn • has pest control • pleasing appearance	• closing can be difficult depending on model and fullness of bin
Door (small at bottom)	• suited to ever-producing compost • easy to access finished compost at bottom	• not suitable for hot compost method and turning

Many of the commercial composting units have a little door at the bottom for easy access to the finished compost. You may need to purchase a special narrow shovel to fit through the door. It takes a while for the initial batch of compost to be ready, but once it is, you'll have a constant supply for your potted plants and for top-dressing your garden. Check out the Aeration Composter Unit Building Plans section (p. 48) for diagrams on how to build your own single-bin compost system, and see the Aeration Composter Units Available for Purchase section (p. 50) for a review of commercial models available on the market.

Three-bin Bertha: big and beautiful

If you have a big yard, consider the three-bin composter. The three-bin system is made to hold a hot, active pile of composting waste in one bin and a storage pile of fresh waste that you are adding to in another, with an empty bin left over. Why the empty bin? Well, mixing a big pile of yard waste with a shovel is really hard to do. Instead, try shovelling the decomposing waste from one bin to the empty one. The action of shovelling adds air to the pile and mixes up the contents— kind of like shuffling a deck of cards. Depending on how you build your three-bin system, it can be a quick job to shuffle

Single-bin unit

Three-bin unit

the active pile back and forth every week or so. It is also a great opportunity to make sure the stuff on the outside edges of the pile gets turned into the middle so the pile decomposes evenly. Three-bin composting is a hot batch composting process that can produce compost in less than one month.

The cost of putting together a three-bin composter depends on how beautiful you want it to be. There are no set rules stating that it has to be made from perfectly constructed wood panels with a hinged lid and removable doors. The main idea is to have room for a fresh waste pile and an active pile, and someplace to move it back and forth. The easiest, cheapest way is to have no bin at all—just make the piles out in the open. However, most people like to protect their piles from the elements, so they construct a holding unit. One cheap, easy way to make a nice three-bin

composter is to nail or tie seven same-sized, untreated wood pallets together to act as walls. You could even grab a few more and use hinges to attach them like doors or to use as a raised floor. The slats in the pallets are great for making sure air gets to the pile.

Three-bin Composting Units

✓ Are great for hot composting

✓ Handle large volumes of waste

✓ Produce compost quickly

✓ Make it easy to keep track of your turning schedule

✓ Protect against some pests and the elements (when a lid and front doors are added)

✗ Require a large space

✗ Require a strong back for shovelling dirt back and forth

Many industries are happy to give away their old, used pallets. Take a trip out to the dump one day, and you will likely see a load of them coming in. Though many community landfills have bylaws against scavenging, you can ask around for the name or contact info of the regular "donors" and offer to save them a trip the next time out. Even better, if they are not finished unloading, you can offer to take some of the load off their hands, saving them some dumping costs.

Other possible bin construction materials include cement cinder blocks piled in the shape you need, plywood sheets or a wooden frame with chicken wire mesh to hold the compost in place. If you like to build things, check out the Aeration Composter Unit Building Plans section (p. 48) for a diagram on how to build your own three-bin compost system.

Rotating Batch Unit

The easiest way to get quick hot compost is to throw your wastes in a rotating composter. You can buy one of the commercial models available or make your own unit using an old garbage can with a lid or a 170 L drum. All you need to do is drill some holes in a big container, fill it three-quarters full of mixed green and brown waste and roll it around your yard every week. Better yet, you could put an axle through the middle of the barrel and rotate it in place, like a bingo machine. You can get finished compost in less than one month without the backaches of shovelling a traditional composting unit.

Keep in mind that a rotating composter is a batch system where you have to have a large quantity of prepared waste before you start. The composter is not meant to handle a regular addition of

Rotating batch unit

materials, so you have to find a place to store your wastes until your batch is finished or until you have enough to fill the unit. Think of it like baking a cake—you have to prepare the batter beforehand, throw it in the oven and let the oven do its work. A cake will not cook properly if you keep adding flour and other ingredients while it is in the oven cooking. A rotating batch will not compost evenly if you keep adding wastes all the time.

Building your own rotating unit out of reused supplies can be cheap, but buying a commercial model can be fairly expensive. See the Aeration Composter Unit Building Plans section (p. 48) for a diagram on how to build your own rotating compost system, and see the Aeration Composter Units Available for Purchase section (p. 50) for a review of commercial models available on the market.

Rotating Batch Composting Units

✓ Use a hot composting method
✓ Produce compost quickly
✓ Protect against pests
✓ Are easy to mix
✗ Require large amounts of wastes all at once
✗ Cannot be added to while they are processing

No matter how it's made, compost will help you make your garden beautiful.

Aeration Composter Unit Building Plans

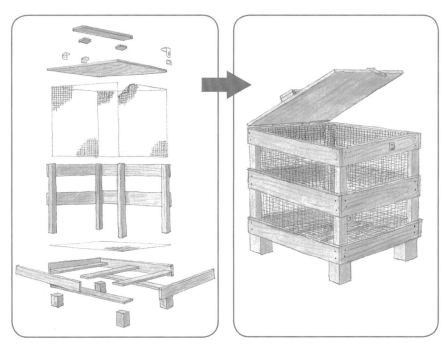

Single-bin unit

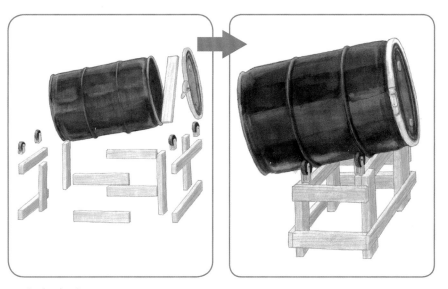

Rotating batch unit

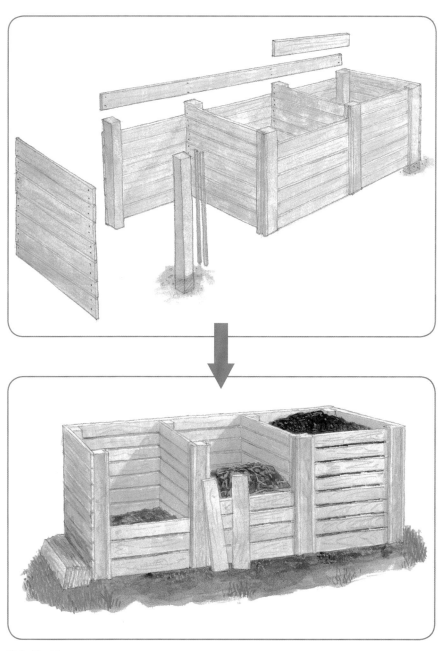

Three-bin unit

Aeration Composter Units Available for Purchase

Many manufactured composting units are available for purchase in Canada. These units are great if you are not handy with wood and tools or you just don't have the time or energy to build one from scratch. The units mentioned here are just a few examples of what is available in stores and online. Not all compost units are created equal, so a rough review that touches on customer opinions is described below. For more information about these or any composter, use the internet to search out customer reviews and suggestions before purchasing any bin.

Garden Gourmet

This compost unit has many knock-off generic brand units that are available at

Garden Gourmet

most hardware stores as well as online. Shop around to find the best price, because many different companies produce this bin.

You have to assemble the Garden Gourmet yourself, but it is a fairly simple task because it snaps together like Lego® blocks and anchors to the ground. It is made of hard, black, recycled plastic, and when placed in a sunny location, it heats up nicely.

This unit is tall and narrow, which makes it fit neatly in small nooks and corners. Flap doors make dumping in materials easy, and a small door at the bottom allows access to the finished compost. This composter has a peaked roof, which consumer reports credit with keeping raccoons out. The lid sheds rain but has small holes at the top to allow a bit of water to get in and keep the pile moist. Small ventilation holes all around the bin aerate the pile while keeping out larger pests and insects.

The Garden Gourmet is good as an ever-producing cold composter. It can handle the kitchen waste of a small family and a small amount of yard waste. However, it is not convenient for hot composting because it is too narrow to provide sufficient insulation for the microorganisms to properly heat up. Also, the height and narrow build of the bin makes mixing or turning awkward.

You need to plan for aeration with this bin or you risk anaerobic conditions. Some consumers have complained that the lid blows off in strong winds. They also warn that warping from pressure and the sun's heat makes rebuilding or relocating the bin difficult. Other consumer complaints involve the door at the bottom of the unit not staying securely fixed to the bin.

Earth Machine

This unit is difficult to find in stores; however, many municipalities sell it at a discounted rate. Call your local compost education or waste management department to see if they have a program to distribute this bin.

The Earth Machine is useful as a cold compost unit. You can produce compost in batches or as ever-producing compost. If you purchase the black plastic model, it will heat up nicely in the summer sun.

You can use the little door at the bottom to remove finished compost if you are making ever-producing compost. If you are making batch compost, the cone shape of the bin allows you to

Earth Machine

easily lift the bin away from its contents when ready. There is a nice locking lid to keep large pests out and pegs to anchor the bin in place.

Some consumers have complained about the fragility of the thin plastic. If the bin is too full and placed in a warm location, the top half can warp away from the bottom half, making the bin impossible to put back together.

SoilSaver

This unit is available in stores and is sold by some municipalities at a subsidized price. Check with your local municipality to see if they have a program for distributing this compost unit.

The SoilSaver is one of the larger compost units and can hold enough waste for hot composting. The heat-generating, black, plastic casing facilitates making a quick hot compost batch. It has a locking lid and aeration holes on the side and top to let in air and small amounts of moisture while keeping most pests out. Two sliding doors at the bottom allow for double the access to the waste in the bin.

Most complaints about this bin refer to how difficult it is to turn the compost while it is still in the bin. One suggested solution is to use the little doors at the bottom to scoop out the undigested wastes and redeposit them on top of the pile. You can also remove and relocate the bin beside its current location and refill it with the partially digested wastes. Some owners have three bins for a makeshift three-bin unit, leaving one empty, one active and one for storage of new wastes.

The SoilSaver does work as a cold compost unit, but its large holding capacity can easily lead to compression and anaerobic conditions. Plan for aeration with this bin if you want ever-producing compost.

Also, be sure to situate this unit on level ground because the lid does not fit or lock in place otherwise, making the contents vulnerable to pests such as raccoons and decreasing the lifespan of the bin.

SoilSaver

NatureMill Automatic Composter

This is one of the few (possibly only) indoor aerobic models available on the market. It is moderately expensive but is perhaps worth the cost if you cannot compost outdoors.

This small bin is the size of a garbage can that can fit under the sink or in a cupboard. You feed it kitchen wastes (including meats and cheese) and sawdust pellets as a mix of greens and browns. Two hot, rotating rods mix the waste, and it produces finished compost in two weeks. When the compost is ready, it falls into a tray that you can empty into your garden. The composter comes with its own biological activator that you need to use only once—the first time you use the unit—so you don't need to clean the bin, or you will kill off the bacteria culture.

Consumer reports indicate that the tight-fitting lid and fast composting action prevents fruit flies and unpleasant smells. However, the unit can be very noisy, especially in the first couple weeks of ownership—so be prepared for loud banging noises in the night. As the unit ages and works out its kinks, it quiets down.

Sun-Mar Garden Composter

This rotating tumbler unit is not a batch system; it is actually an ever-producing composter and can handle everyday kitchen wastes and a small amount of yard wastes. It has a unique internal cylinder that gathers finished compost in the middle and leaves undigested wastes in the bin. It also protects against pests and smells and, at first glance, seems fairly easy to use.

This unit has received both positive and negative consumer reports. People who have had success with this tumbler fill it as full as they can with a mix of green and brown waste, moisten it and rotate the barrel once a week. Once the bin is full, a mix of brown and green wastes can be continuously added to produce compost consistently.

Many complaints about this unit have to do with its high cost and the slow production of compost for people who do not have a large volume of waste. These customers find that the unit takes a long time to produce finished compost because the bin needs to be full before it will unload out the inner spout. Other consumer complaints include having the inner spout break loose from the composter and needing replacement parts.

Wire Compost Bin

As either homemade or purchased models, these bins are fairly inexpensive. When making your own bin, do not use chicken wire because larger pests and mice can chew through it. Use steel mesh or hardware cloth instead. The models available for purchase are nice because they come with long metal pins to give the bin structure and to anchor it to the ground.

This style of bin is best for yard wastes because it does not protect against many animals. If pests are

Wire compost bin

not a concern for you, you can try composting kitchen wastes in it as well. It also does not protect against heat, wind or rain, so monitor moisture levels carefully.

The best feature of this unit is that it is very mobile: you can take it apart and put it back together easily. It is also easy to turn and mix, like an open pile, but stays neat and contained the rest of the time. Most of these units (either round or square) can be adjusted for size depending on whether you want to do hot or cold composting.

Corner Rod Composter

This is a partly manufactured, partly homemade compost unit. You purchase wooden slats in the length of your choice to construct a square bin with large spaces for ventilation, then anchor the wood together with the manufactured Compost Corner Rods. The corner rods make construction fairly simple once the slats have been cut to size.

The corner rod composter can be relatively expensive once you factor in the cost of purchasing the wood and the corner pieces, as well as spending time constructing the unit.

Composting with this unit is best for large volumes of yard wastes. Depending on how big you build it, you can do either hot or cold composting. This unit does not have a lid, so you need to monitor moisture levels. It is fairly solid, but you can leave one side of the bin unanchored to the corners so that you can get in and turn

the pile. If you want to compost kitchen wastes, keep in mind that although the unit is a bit sturdier than a wire unit for keeping animals out, raccoons, mice and rats can easily access the pile from above, below or in between the slats.

Rotating Composter

There are many different models of rotating units. On average, rotating units are more expensive than single-bin units. Look for a bin that will be easy to rotate when it is three-quarters full. Some of the large units in an upright barrel design can be difficult to turn over when close to being full. Units with an axel on the inside are good because the bar breaks up clumps of compost. However, if you leave the compost unit too long without turning it, the pile will compress into a block, slide from the end of the composter to the bar, and get stuck there. The same is true for almost all tumbler units: if you don't turn them regularly, you will have trouble with clumping and sliding rather than getting an even mix. A rotating barrel is a great purchase if you are willing to pay a bit more, and if you know you will rotate the barrel one or two times per week. Also remember, it is a batch unit. You fill it three-quarters full and don't add anymore until it is ready to harvest. Some of the smaller units have compost tea collection containers at the bottom. Make sure the unit you buy has air holes, or you will likely get anaerobic conditions.

Situating Your Bin

A compost pile is a delicate mini-ecosystem that supports billions of organisms in a web of life. Choose a location for your composter that gives you the most control over the environmental conditions of the pile. First, you need to evaluate your local climate so that you can plan to mediate the effects of outside influences on the moisture and heat levels of your compost pile. Do you live in a humid coastal city like Victoria or Halifax? Or is your climate dry and sunny like the hoodoos in southern Alberta? Does your yard face north and get little sun, or does it face south and experience blazing heat all summer long? The moisture levels in the air and the amount of sun in your yard are important to the success of your bin. You need to balance the warming power of the sun, which increases microbial activity, with evaporation, which dries out your pile. People who live in a cool, humid environment right next to the coast or a lake often have piles that get and stay too wet. Overly wet piles tend to lack oxygen and turn anaerobic easily. They also stay cool, which is a problem if you want to try hot composting. One solution is to place your pile in a location in your yard that gets a lot of sun exposure. You will have an easier job of aerating your pile and letting it warm up so the microbes can do their job.

In an environment where the soil and air are very hot and dry, you may want to set your pile in a shaded, sheltered area out of the intense summer

Consider environmental conditions, garden layout and neighbours when deciding on a location for your compost pile.

sun. If you leave a pile out to bake, it will lose all its moisture. Without regular watering, your compost pile will dry out, killing many of the beneficial bacteria that are working to break down your waste. Bacteria and fungi need moisture to live, so a dry pile is inactive and takes a long time to decompose.

Similarly, if you live in a location that gets a lot of wind, consider a sheltered location for your bin and be sure to keep the lid or cover on your pile so the contents don't dry out too quickly.

Place your composter in a level, well-drained area over dirt or grass. Healthy compost piles leach out nutrient-rich water from the bottom of the pile, so keep your composter off driveways or concrete pads. Keeping the pile over soil also encourages worms and other decomposers to access the pile from below.

How you plan to use the compost pile will determine where you locate it. If you want finished compost in less than one month and are prepared to work at the pile, situate your composter in a place where you have room to move around. Place it close to the garden in which you plan to use the finished product so that you don't have to haul it across the yard. Some people place their compost piles right on an unused corner of their garden to make moving finished compost really easy.

If you are happy to wait a whole season before you get some finished compost and you just want to throw in your kitchen scraps on a regular basis while pulling out small shovelfuls of finished compost from the bottom of the unit every once in a while, you may consider situating your pile close to or within easy reach of your back door. The convenience of having a unit nearby is particularly appealing in winter so you don't have to trek through snow to dump out your pail of kitchen scraps.

Sometimes compost piles can sit in a yard for so long that you forget they are there, and they become part of the scenery. If you know you are a lazy gardener, situate your pile in a place where you can't miss it, close to where you will be working, so that you remember to check the pile for aeration and moisture levels.

Lastly, be conscious of your relationship with your neighbours. If you have a fragile relationship with the people next door, consider placing the bin along your back fence, where accidental smells or a fly infestation won't start a feud. Keep your pile away from a spot along a fence directly adjacent to where your neighbours have a patio or barbecue set up. As well, not everyone likes the look of an open compost pile. If your neighbour's yard overlooks your own, a neatly enclosed compost unit, rather than an open pile, might be best.

Earth knows no desolation.
She smells regeneration in the moist breath of decay.

–George Meredith

What to Put in Your Pile

Like all living creatures, decomposers need a mixed diet from different food groups to thrive. With a balanced diet, the microorganisms will break down your pile quickly with few problems. If you do not have a balanced feedstock, you will encounter symptoms of poor composter health, such as smells, slow decomposition or a pile that does not heat up.

The microorganisms in your pile require two basic nutrients to thrive: nitrogen and carbon. The good news is that every living or once-living thing on earth contains both nitrogen and carbon. Nitrogen is the basic building block for microorganisms to reproduce and grow. The more nitrogen you have in your pile, the more decomposers you will have. Carbon is the basic food for decomposers. The more carbon you have, the healthier they will be. Composting enthusiasts refer to high-nitrogen materials as greens and high-carbon materials as browns.

Fresh wastes from your kitchen and yard are feedstocks that are high in nitrogen. Some "greens" are green in colour, such as freshly cut grass,

Make sure you add only suitable materials to your compost pile.

but some are not, such as coffee grounds or manure from herbivorous animals. Feedstocks that are higher in carbon are usually dead and dry. Brown leaves in autumn, straw and paper are a few examples. These high-carbon materials still have a small quantity of nitrogen in them, but not much.

The bad news is that too much carbon or nitrogen puts your pile out of balance and limits the microorganisms' ability to quickly decompose the matter. If there is too much nitrogen for the microorganisms to use, it can undergo a chemical reaction and be released into the air as ammonia. If you can smell the ammonia, which has an unpleasant odour, and if you notice your pile has turned at least partly into green sludge, your pile has too much nitrogen. If you have too much carbon, the pile will not heat up or will decompose very slowly.

The ideal ratio of carbon to nitrogen is 30:1. However, without special soil testing equipment and know-how, you won't be able to attain the perfect nitrogen to carbon ratio. When you mix equal weights of fresh, green materials with dead, brown materials, the carbon to nitrogen ratio usually balances out between an acceptable range of 20:1 to 40:1. However, if you want great results, aim to get as close as you can to a 30:1 ratio.

Most gardeners are not scientists with high-tech compost testing equipment. If you are curious about the carbon ratio of your compost, send a finished batch to your local university soil specialist or soil professional. But if

you are like the rest of us, you are probably content to just wing it. With a general idea of which materials are high in nitrogen and which are low, you can guess at appropriate weights of each going into your pile. For example, usually you want to add half dead, brown material and half fresh, green materials. Certain dry, brown materials, such as paper, sawdust and wood chips, are especially low in nitrogen, so you may need to put in fresh waste that is really high in nitrogen, such as chicken manure or blood meal, to compensate. The list on the facing page shows the most common compost feedstocks and their carbon to nitrogen ratios.

Basic Carbon to Nitrogen Ratio Math

Calculating an approximate carbon ratio is possible using the table on page 59. Just add the carbon values, add the nitrogen values and then divide the two. For example, take one part kitchen waste (approx. C:N is 10:1), one part fresh grass clippings (approx. C:N is 15:1) and one part dead leaves (approx. C:N is 60:1). Add the values and you have 85 parts carbon (10+15+60) and 3 parts nitrogen (1+1+1), and you have a carbon to nitrogen ratio of 28.3:1 (85:3). This ratio is pretty close to 30:1 but is slightly high in nitrogen. Consider balancing out the carbon by mixing in a bucket of finished compost or dirt to inoculate the pile, and you will have a well-balanced feedstock.

Remember, you need to accommodate how much feedstock you use in

Carbon to Nitrogen Ratios of Feedstock

Material	Carbon:Nitrogen
Dead leaves	40:1 to 80:1
Newsprint	400:1 to 850:1
Paper	170:1
Wood chips	500:1 to 700:1
Corrugated cardboard	560:1
Sawdust	150:1 to 500:1
Corn stalks	60:1
Dry straw	96:1
Kitchen scraps	10:1 to 15:1
Coffee grounds	25:1
Fresh garden waste	20:1
Vegetable waste	12:1
Fresh weeds	20:1
Fresh grass clippings	15:1
Fresh cow manure	20:1
Fresh horse manure	35:1
Blood meal	3:1
Soybean meal	7:1
Hay	15:1 to 32:1

Carbon to nitrogen ratios of some common compost feedstocks as calculated by weight. The feedstocks in the brown section are high in carbon; the feedstocks in the green area are high in nitrogen.

your calculations. If you used one part dead leaves and one part greens (half grass, half kitchen scraps) the calculation would be 85 parts carbon divided by 2 parts nitrogen (1+0.5+0.5), which equals a carbon to nitrogen ratio of 42.5:1. If you forget to account for the quantity of each feedstock, your calculations will be incorrect.

As another example, if you put one handful of blood meal (approx. C:N is 3:1) with a barrel of dry straw (approx. C:N is 96:1), you will not have one part blood meal and one part straw, you will have one part blood meal and about 500 parts straw. Your calculations should be

$96(500)+ 3(1)=48003$ divided by $500(1)+1(1)= 501$, equalling a high carbon to nitrogen ratio of 95.8:1, which would result in a pile that fails to heat up and decomposes very slowly unless high-nitrogen material were added to balance the pile.

This very basic calculation system is not exact and does not accommodate for bioavailability, density or moisture levels, which are other major factors in achieving a healthy compost pile. The exact calculations of carbon to nitrogen ratios are complex, and the above calculations should be used only as a rough guideline.

Popular Feedstocks

The items listed in the carbon to nitrogen ratio table are not the only items that can go into your compost bin. If it was once alive and growing, it can decompose. However, for planned healthy composting, it helps to know a bit about what you are putting in and what effect it will have on the pile. Some feedstocks decompose more quickly than others and some can alter the pH, moisture and porosity of your pile. It also helps to know which feedstocks can be harmful or troublesome so you can keep them out of your pile.

Appropriate Household Wastes

Breads and pastas: Experiment with plain breads and cooked or dry pasta in your compost pile in moderation as long as they are not fatty (like muffins) or coated with fat, cream or meat sauce (like peanut butter and jelly or alfredo sauce with meatballs). Bury the plain pasta or bread at least 15 cm deep in your pile. If you have problems with pests in your area (such as raccoons or rats), keep these items out of your pile.

Clamshells: Like eggshells, these are high in calcium and are good for the soil and compost. However, they decompose slowly, and you may be best off crushing them with a hammer over a cement pad. They are useful for adding air pockets to the soil and for providing habitat for the decomposers in the pile. Don't put too many in a pile, though, or they will be more of a hassle than they are worth.

Coffee grounds are acidic, so add them in moderation.

Coffee grounds: The grounds and filter are acceptable feedstocks, but be careful not to use too much because coffee is acidic and will affect the pH of your compost. Coffee grounds can be directly mixed into the soil around plants that require acidic soil or mixed with a small amount of lime to neutralize the pH. They are also a favourite worm food, but bury the coffee completely or mix it with other wastes because it can sometimes attract fruit flies.

Corncobs: These are notoriously hard to compost. Chop them up to speed decomposition. If they are not finished decomposing by the end of your first batch of compost, screen them out, chop them up more and add them to the next batch.

Eggshells: Whole eggshells take a very long time to break down. However, if you finely chop, crush or grind them into a powder, they are a great source of calcium for compost or soil—especially around tomato plants. Eggshells are also slightly alkaline and can be used to neutralize the acidity of coffee grounds or citrus rinds. Rinse the eggshells to minimize the risk of salmonella infection. Simple methods of preparing the shells include putting dry shells in a blender or food processor, mincing them with a sturdy vegetable knife or sealing them in a plastic bag and crushing them with a rolling pin.

Floor sweepings, vacuum dust and dryer lint: Most dust and floor sweepings are organic materials that will decompose, such as food, skin, hair and pet fur particles. Dryer lint may not be good for your compost bin if you use chemical dryer sheets. Consider using dryer balls if you plan on composting the lint. Lint from synthetic fabrics, such as polyester and nylon, won't decompose. Spread the contents of a vacuum bag to prevent matting. Some inorganic material will likely get sucked up by the vacuum and will not decompose but should have a neutral effect on the soil and compost pile.

Fruit peels and waste: Do not use too many citrus fruit wastes, such as orange and lemon peels, all at once because they will affect the acidity of the pile. Chop up large fruit, such as watermelon rinds, to increase the surface area for easier decomposition. Certain fruit peels, such as bananas and peaches, carry the microscopic eggs of fruit flies. Bury the peels at least 10 cm deep so that the flies do not infest your pile.

Hair and pet fur: High in nitrogen, human hair and pet fur are great for the compost pile. Break up big clumps of hair and fur and mix them into the pile. However, hair decomposes slowly, and if you use many chemical products on your hair, leave it out of the pile.

Herbivorous animal feces and bedding: Pet hamster, guinea pig, mouse and rabbit feces and the shavings the animals live in can be safely composted in a hot pile. Layer the shavings thinly in your pile to prevent matting. Human, bird and carnivorous animal (dog and cat) wastes are not acceptable for your compost pile.

Houseplants: The soil and remains of indoor potted plants are great for your composter as long as they are free from chemical treatments, disease, infection or pest infestations. Throw infected plants in the garbage and sterilize the pot before you reuse it.

Tomato wastes are appropriate.

Peanut shells can be added but may need to go through several compost batches.

Human urine: Sterile and very high in nitrogen (C:N ratio of 7:1), human urine is a great compost activator for a slowly decomposing pile. Be sure the urine donor is in good health with no kidney or liver disorders, and it will be safe to use. Mix the urine into the pile or it may smell, and the nitrogen will evaporate if the urine is simply drizzled on top of the pile. Urine is high in salt, so don't use it directly on the garden, or you risk burning your plants.

Natural fabrics: Cotton, silk, linen, wool, ramie and hemp are fabrics made from plant fibres. Shred the fabrics thoroughly, make sure they are mixed well with other materials in the pile and keep them moist. If you suspect the dye on the fabric is chemical rather than natural, you may not want to add the fabric to the pile. Fabrics are not common feedstocks for home compost piles; consider reusing old shirts for rags instead. Fabric soaked in oil, paint or chemicals is not appropriate for the compost pile.

Nut and seed shells: These decompose slowly, so mix them thoroughly with high-nitrogen kitchen scraps. If the shells were salted, give them a soak to dissolve the salts and moisten them for faster decomposition. Expect to screen out and reinsert shells through a series of compost batches before they decompose completely.

Oatmeal, flours and low-fat and low-sugar cereals: If the oatmeal has not been mixed with sugar or fat, you can compost it safely. Bran and cereals that have little to no sugar are acceptable as well. Small amounts of flour can be mixed in the compost pile but will mat and negatively affect pile aeration, porosity and drainage if left in layers or clumps. Bury these items under at least 15 cm of dry, brown waste in the pile or leave them out altogether if you are concerned that you might attract animals (such as raccoons or dogs).

Paper and cardboard: Newspaper and many office paper inks are made from vegetable based oils. You can safely compost these papers without concern that mineral or chemical toxicity will build in your pile. However, the ink/toner used on magazine, flyer and copy paper is often full of chemicals that could disrupt the delicate life cycles of the creatures in your pile. Shred any paper or cardboard you plan to compost because it tends to mat and break down slowly if you put it in the pile as whole sheets. Recycle paper with questionable ink instead of putting it in your pile.

Pet foods: Spoiled pet foods made of cornmeal, soybeans, alfalfa and canola meal are high sources of nitrogen that work great as starters to get your pile heated up quickly. Examples are cheap, dry dog and cat food, chicken feed and rabbit feed. Birdseed should be composted with caution and only in a hot composter because the seeds could germinate in the composter, creating weeds in your pile. In areas where large pests, such as raccoons, are a problem, be sure to bury the food near the centre of the pile with at least 15 cm of other feedstocks covering it.

Tea leaves: Tea bags and leaves are biodegradable; expect to find a few staples left after decomposition.

Vegetable peels and waste: Chop whole, large vegetables, such as squash, sweet potatoes and cucumber, to help the microorganisms get past the hard skin and speed up the composting process. Corn husks break down slowly and need to be finely chopped or put through several batches of compost before they fully decompose.

Wet paper towels: If the paper towels are not full of fat, milk or meat wastes, you can safely add them to your compost pile. Tissues are okay as long as they don't contain fluids from sick individuals.

Chop up vegetable wastes before adding them.

Appropriate Garden Wastes

Acidic material: Oak leaves, pine needles, etc. are highly acidic and will affect the pH of your compost pile. Some plants, such as blueberries, thrive in acidic soil. You can make a special pile especially for acid-loving plants, or you can neutralize the acidic pH by sprinkling in small amounts of alkaline materials, such as wood ashes or limestone. Pine needles break down slowly, so shred them and balance their decomposition with a high-nitrogen material like blood meal or manure to ensure faster decomposition.

Dead plants and plant waste: Old annuals, legumes, vines and other wastes from the yard cleanup are acceptable. Chop them for a healthy mix of greens for your pile.

Grass clippings and sod: Grass-cycling (leaving grass on the lawn) is the best way to deal with grass clippings. However, if you need a ready source of high-nitrogen feedstock, add the clippings to your compost pile instead. Make sure the layers of grass are not too thick in your pile (no more than 5 cm) or you could get clumping and ammonia smells. Sod decomposes nicely. Layer it dirt side up to make sure the roots die out and so the top of the pile is covered with a dirt layer. Mix it with a carbonaceous material, such as dead leaves or straw, to balance the high nitrogen content of the pile.

Add pine needles in moderation.

Sod is a good source of nitrogen.

Autumn leaves are an excellent addition.

Weeds are a safe addition as long as they haven't gone to seed.

Leaves: Leaves are one of the few feedstocks that can be composted alone or with a small addition of a high-nitrogen product, such as blood meal. Composted leaves are called leaf mould and are slightly acidic, but when used as part of a balanced feedstock for your compost pile, their acidity is not a major concern. Use a mower to chop leaves for fast decomposition.

Soil: Though it is mostly inorganic and does not break down, a small quantity of soil will add microorganisms to your pile and provide structure and habitat for them.

Weeds: As long as weeds have not started seeding, they can safely go into a compost pile. As an extra precaution, let them dry out and die in the sun before mixing them into your pile. Guinea pigs also really like to eat weeds, and you can use their high-nitrogen manure in your compost instead of putting the weeds directly in the pile. Leave out weeds that germinate from their leaves or roots, such as quack grass, bishop's weed, bittersweet, etc. If you find weeds growing on your pile, their seeds likely blew in from outside the pile. Turn them into the centre of your pile to decompose them. Remove any weeds you find growing in your finished compost before you spread it in your garden, or place the compost in a bucket and let it sit in the hot sun for up to one month to kill any weeds that survived the composting process.

External Sources of Feedstock

If you feel passionate about composting but don't produce enough feedstock in your own yard to make compost, you can acquire compost feedstock from local farms and industries where organic waste is plentiful. Owners are usually more than happy to give it away for free or at low cost.

Alfalfa: Green manure or cover crops are made from alfalfa because it is high in nitrogen and it composts easily. Purchasing alfalfa hay can be expensive, and you are better off buying it in the pellet form used as feedstock for animals. You can also check with farmers for rotted bales that they may be willing to give you.

Blood meal: Found at most garden centres, blood meal is high in nitrogen and acts as a good compost starter. Mix blood meal in with leaves for quick and hot production of leaf mould compost.

Bone meal: A by-product of the meat processing industry, bone meal is high in phosphorus and nitrogen. You should be able to find it for sale at garden centres.

Feathers: Chicken farmers and poultry processing plants often have feather waste. It is high in nitrogen and composts well when mixed with other wastes.

Hay: Many farmers are happy to offload half-rotted hay for free or for the cost of delivery. Though it is high in

Local farms are a good source of compost feedstock.

A fool looks for dung where the cow never browsed.

–Ethiopian proverb

nitrogen, hay can be treated like a brown, carbonaceous material and mixed with high-nitrogen materials. Hay is often contaminated with weeds, so it is a good idea to hot compost it before it is used in the garden. To prevent matting in your pile, spread layers of hay thinly or shred the hay using a shredding machine or by running over shallow mats with a lawn mower.

Hoof and horn meal: This is cheaper to purchase from stores than blood meal and does as good a job. Be sure to purchase the fine dust form and avoid the granular form, which can attract flies and does not break down easily.

Industrial organic wastes: Explore local industries for organic wastes such as buckwheat hulls, sugar wastes, tankage, tobacco wastes, wool wastes, apple pomace, etc. Many industries pay to dispose of these wastes and will happily give you as much as you would like to save the cost of disposal. Be sure to investigate the nature of the product (e.g. the mineral content and carbon to nitrogen ratios) before putting these items in your pile. *The Rodale Book of Composting* has great information on many compostable industrial wastes. Only use wastes from local industries—it makes no sense to pollute the air by shipping waste across the continent.

Lime: Useful if you have acidic feedstock, lime will increase the pH of your compost. Use it sparingly because it can react with nitrogen to form ammonia and result in a loss of nitrogen into the air.

Hay is often full of weed seeds and is best hot composted.

Manure: Touted as two of the most important sources of nitrogen for a hot compost pile, manure and urine from herbivorous animals such as chickens, cows, goats and horses are excellent sources of long-lasting nitrogen. Manure is also full of the microorganisms needed for composting. Sources of manure include local farms, equestrian schools, zoos and anywhere livestock are housed. Compost fresh manure as soon as possible so that it doesn't lose nitrogen into the air.

Peat moss: This is an arguably non-renewable natural resource that is losing popularity with many gardeners. Peat forms over thousands of years as organic matter breaks down in bogs and wetlands. Researchers are trying to find a way to speed up the production of peat, but in the meantime, wildlife supported by the bogs suffers the consequences of peat mining. Peat can be purchased at garden centres and used as a high-carbon material for your compost pile. It is often acidic, so you may want to consult the staff where you purchase it for more information before using it with acid-sensitive plants. Peat is often used in potting mixes from garden centres; however, finished compost is a better, cheaper alternative for making your own potting mix.

Sawdust: Extremely high in carbon, sawdust decomposes when mixed with a high-nitrogen feedstock, such as manure. Do not use sawdust from treated wood or particleboard. Mix sawdust in thoroughly with other ingredients to prevent matting. Sawdust can be used as a mulch, though you should pre-treat the soil below with organic

Manure is an excellent source of nitrogen.

fertilizer to prevent the sawdust from drawing nitrogen away from the soil.

Seaweed: The micronutrient content of seaweed or packaged dried seaweed (kelp meal) is very high. Seaweed is high in nitrogen as well and acts as a great compost activator. Wet seaweed loses its nutrients quickly when exposed to the elements, so mix it into your compost as soon as possible or soak it in water to make a seaweed tea for your garden or compost pile.

Straw: Straw is low in nitrogen so it needs a high-nitrogen material, such as manure, to compost quickly. Straw shafts provide great aeration but tend to dry the pile out easily.

Wood chips: Much like sawdust, wood chips are high in carbon and are difficult to break down. Use fresh wood chips as a mulch around plants and in the garden. After a year or two, when the wood chips begin to lose their colour and start to soften, put them in a compost heap mixed with a high-nitrogen material, such as manure. The large particle size adds porosity and aeration to the pile. Do not compost wood chips that are made from treated wood or have heavy chemical dyes.

Use wood chips as mulch before you add them to your compost pile.

Inappropriate Household Wastes

Carnivorous pet or human feces:
Animals that have meat in their diets, such as dogs, cats and humans, excrete pathogens in their feces. Bird feces also has pathogens. Pathogens are harmful bacteria that cause disease; you do not want them in your garden. Only commercial compost piles that consistently heat up past 72° C for at least three days can guarantee to kill pathogens. Home compost units do not compost hot enough or for long enough to ensure all pathogens are killed, so leave these types of feces out of your pile.

Chemicals and cleaning agents:
Antibacterial soaps are not good for a compost pile, which requires working bacteria. Household cleaners and chemical products are not good either. Take chemical items to a local hazardous waste handler such as a toxic roundup or Eco Station, and leave them out of your compost bin.

Cigarette butts: Nicotine acts as a natural pesticide and will kill many of the beneficial organisms in your pile. The filter is not easily biodegradable andcan take from 10 to 80 years to decompose.

Fats: Fatty material often smells rancid and attracts animals as it decomposes. It also coats particles in your pile, affecting aeration and moisture content,

Do not add dog feces to your pile.

which sometimes causes anaerobic conditions. Some sealed anaerobic digester composter models can handle small amounts of fat, but you should leave it out of any other kind of composter.

Inorganics: It seems obvious, but the beginner composter may not know—plastics, glass, metals, cement and rock are not compostable. You do not have to worry about their accidental presence in your pile or garden in small quantities, such as staples from a tea bag or a little bit of plastic. However, do not deliberately put them in your pile because they affect porosity, and chemicals from plastic can seep into the composting material. Laying gravel for drainage at the bottom of your pile is okay, but adding tiles or cement blocks from a renovation is not a good idea and will make turning and aerating difficult.

Leather: Leather products could probably decompose nicely but are safe to use in your compost pile only if they have not been treated with chemicals. The tanning process often uses heavy minerals, such as chromium, that can be harmful to the decomposers, the garden and you. Unless you know how the leather was treated during manufacturing, leave it out of your pile.

Meat and bones: Bones are a great source of phosphoric acids and calcium but may take a long time to decompose. Think of dinosaurs and ask yourself if you have that kind of time. As well, bones attract animals and pests. Bones that have been softened in a soup may decompose more readily but must be placed in a bin that is secure from pets and pests. Meat attracts animals and flies. Meat and bones can be composted in an anaerobic digester but should not be put in an aerobic pile.

Milk products: Cream, cheese, yogourt, sour cream and other milk products are not good items for your compost feedstock. Sour milk products smell awful and will attract animals from all over the neighbourhood. The fats in milk products affect microorganisms' access to moisture and air and may turn your pile anaerobic. Some anaerobic digesters can compost milk products, but leave these products out of an aerobic compost pile.

Sugars: Sugars decompose, but you risk attracting pests to your pile. Ants in particular love sugary treats and will build a home in your pile if they detect the slightest trace of refined sugar.

Whole eggs: Once cracked, the yolk and white may attract pests, smell awful and contain harmful bacteria, such as salmonella. Eggs can be composted in certain anaerobic digesters, but they should not go into a regular bin.

Wood ashes: Though they are a great source of potash and potassium for your compost pile or soil, wood ashes are alkaline and high in salt. They should be used sparingly, if at all, in your compost bin or garden so that you don't drastically change the pH and nutrient balance of your pile or soil. Store wood ashes in a dry location—they will dissolve into your soil if left out in the rain.

Inappropriate Garden Wastes

Charcoal and briquettes: Many of these products are inorganic and chemically treated. They can negatively affect the pH and nutrition balance of the compost pile, so leave them out.

Chemicals: Paint, oil, fertilizer and other chemicals that you find in your shed are not appropriate for a healthy compost pile. These items belong at a local hazardous waste collection site.

Diseased plants and soil: Keep diseased plants out of the compost bin to prevent spreading the illness around your garden.

Do not add diseased plants.

Corn stalks are not an ideal addition.

Large, slow-decomposing materials: Whole corn stalks, wood, whole bushes, cardboard boxes and shells decompose slowly and get in the way when you turn your pile. You can add them as part of a planned cold composting aeration technique, but shred or chop them first if you want to try hot composting them. Even when they are finely chopped, you will have to screen these items out of several batches of compost before they fully decompose, so they may be more trouble than they are worth.

Plants treated with chemicals: Herbicides, pesticides, fungicides, etc. are not good for the bacteria in your pile. Leave out any plants that have been treated with chemicals. If you are using waste from a neighbour's yard (grass

Rhubarb leaves may poison your compost pile.

clippings, for example), make sure you know how they manage their plants and control weeds before adding their waste to your pile.

Rhubarb leaves: These leaves are poisonous to most creatures. Rhubarb leaves can be used as a landscaping fabric or mulch, but many gardeners shy away from using them in their compost for fear of poisoning the compost pile and hurting their plants. Feel free to experiment with rhubarb leaves in your compost pile. Some gardeners have success composting rhubarb leaves, while others do not. Boiling the leaves in water and using the juice in a spray bottle is a great natural pesticide for getting rid of aphid infestations and other plant pests in your garden.

Seeded weeds: If they have gone to seed, weeds should be kept out of a compost bin. If you like to take risks, you can try adding them to hot compost bins, which do have some success killing weed seeds, but for the regular cold compost pile, you cannot guarantee that the pile will kill the weeds, and you may end up spreading weeds around your garden.

Balancing Surface Area

When you chop the material you put in your pile, you give the microorganisms greater access to eat it, thus speeding up decomposition. If you chop your material too finely, you risk decreasing the porosity of your pile, losing the air spaces and turning your pile anaerobic. If you don't chop your materials at all, you risk slow or uneven decomposition.

The key is to balance the surface area of the material in your pile. If the material is really fine or powdery, such as sawdust, mix it in small quantities with plenty of chunky materials, such as vegetable scraps or garden waste, so it doesn't clump. Paper has very fine fibres that hold together and compact when wet. Layers of whole sheets of paper will most likely compress and cause problems. To prevent matting, crumple up all paper to make air spaces or pass it through a paper shredder. Before adding it to the pile, mix and coat wet shredded paper with dirt, compost or peat moss while breaking up any clumps.

To quickly and easily chop materials, run a lawn mower over brown leaves or yard wastes. You can also purchase or rent a shredding machine if you expect to have a large volume of wastes to deal with. Remember that chopping your materials will increase the rate of decomposition, but you must stay conscious of the nature of the materials you are putting in. Regular turning and aerating is the best solution for preventing mats or clumps of extra fine materials.

Layering the Feedstock

When creating your pile, make sure you have an even distribution of fresh greens and dry browns. Mix the materials together evenly, or set the greens and browns down in alternating layers that are no more than 7 cm deep. The layers must be thin because if you put all the greens on the bottom and all the browns on the top, your pile will decompose unevenly with smells in one area and inactivity in another. The layers ensure an even mix of materials in your pile.

Water

A healthy compost pile requires just the right amount of water. A pile that is too dry will not decompose. A pile that is too wet will turn anaerobic and start to smell. How do you know what is the right amount of water? When you mix into the pile, the core should be glistening with moisture, but when you grab a handful and squeeze, no water should drip from your hand. Like a wrung-out sponge, the compost should be moist, not sopping wet.

Water is necessary in a pile because microorganisms require moisture to survive. However, if you fill the air spaces with water, the microorganisms won't be able to breathe. A thin coating of water over all the decaying matter in your pile will ensure that the microorganisms can do their job.

If your pile has too much water, turn the compost to expose the water to the air so it can evaporate. You can also add dry materials, such as shredded paper or brown leaves, to absorb the excess moisture. Consider covering your pile with a lid or waterproof fabric to protect it from rain, or move your bin to a sunny location.

If the pile is too dry, there are a number of ways to add water to it. Do not simply pour water on top of it because, often, the pile will shed water from the top down along the sides, and the water won't penetrate the centre of the pile. You will get even water distribution if you water the pile as you turn and mix it. Alternatively, poke a few holes in your pile with an aeration device and water into the holes with a hose. If you set up your pile with an aeration piping system, water into the pipe so that the water reaches the centre of the pile. Another option is to put a weeping hose in the centre of the pile as you build it. Take an old length of hose, drill some holes every few centimetres and plug one end. Turn the hose on every time you think the pile needs watering. Another solution is to give your pile a concave top so that water pools and eventually makes its way into the centre of the pile. Or, take an old pail or milk jug and punch holes a few centimetres up from the bottom so water can seep out to slowly water the pile. If you find that your pile dries out quickly, consider moving it to a shaded location or loosely covering it with a lid or waterproof fabric to trap evaporation.

Make sure you have an even distribution of greens and browns.

Activators

If you see a bag of stuff at your local garden centre that claims to help your pile heat up or work faster, it is likely a compost activator. There are three different categories of activators: bio-activators, mineral activators and nitrogen activators.

Similar to the yeast used as baking, bio-activators are a dry mix of live soil organisms that can be added to a compost pile to inoculate it. In aerobic composting, a bio-activator is not a sensible purchase—not because it doesn't work, but because you can just as easily get it for free (and higher quality) in your own backyard. The hardy bacteria that competed and survived in your yard's topsoil are the most appropriate for your compost bin. The bio-activators you purchase are not likely to survive in your compost pile once they start competing with the native bacteria. If you are really concerned about making sure the "right" bacteria are at work in your pile, use a bit of finished compost or soil as an inoculant as you build your pile.

You can use limestone as a mineral activator.

Mineral activators are not really activators at all—they are soil amendments. Some examples include limestone, rock powders, sulphur and gypsum. These minerals are not necessary in your compost pile and may adversely affect the pile's microbial life. If you are worried that the pH of your pile is too acidic, wait until the compost is finished, do a soil pH test and add a small amount of calcium carbonate to the soil as you mix in the finished compost. Be careful with these mineral additives because you don't want to negatively affect the chemistry of your soil.

Nitrogen activators are the only ones that truly work to get a struggling pile working. If your pile is large enough, moist enough, has the right mix of greens and browns and has been inoculated with soil, it should get hot right away. However, if your pile is not heating up even though you've taken all the necessary steps, you can use an organic nitrogen activator. These are the high-nitrogen feedstocks, such as poultry manure, blood meal, alfalfa pellets and low-grade dog food. Many composting enthusiasts swear by manures as the best way to get a pile hot and steamy.

If you don't want to pay the high prices for organic nitrogen activators at your garden centre, you can often get cheap or free sources of these items from farmers. Be sure to use only organic sources of nitrogen because chemical nitrogen fertilizers will kill the bacteria in your pile.

Ready Compost Recipes

If you are slightly overwhelmed by the number of feedstock options and are unsure of how much of each to use, here are some good recipes to get you started. Once you are comfortable with these recipes, you can experiment by substituting ingredients with similar carbon to nitrogen ratios. These recipes mention particular aeration methods; however, you can adjust the aeration method to suit your personal needs.

Backyard Basics

→ 3 large garbage bags of grass clippings

→ 3 large garbage bags of yard waste

→ 3 large garbage bags of dead, brown leaves

→ 1 x 20 L pail of dirt or finished compost

→ water

→ armful of twigs

Instructions:

1. Scatter twigs at least 7 cm deep at location of new pile.

2. Make alternating layers of leaves, yard waste and clippings with each layer no more than 7 cm thick.

3. Sprinkle soil evenly over each set of three layers.

4. Water the layers.

5. Push a loose bundle of twigs down through the middle of the layers so it makes contact with the twigs beneath.

6. Repeat steps 2, 3 and 4, building layers around the sticks in the middle.

7. Ensure the top layer of the pile is made of leaves and dirt.

8. ■ For cold compost, let the pile sit for up to three months before turning. Water as necessary, and poke with an aeration device every week. Compost will be ready in four to six months.

   ■ For hot compost, turn and water the pile every 7 to 10 days, and leave out the steps involving the twigs, if you choose. Compost will be ready within three to four weeks.

Continual Household Compost

- → 1 x 4 L ice cream pail of kitchen food scraps
- → shredded office paper or newspaper
- → used hamster or rabbit cage shavings and feces
- → stale, cheap dog, cat or rabbit food
- → dirt
- → water
- → aeration device

Instructions:

1. Store a large supply of shredded newspaper, pet food and pet shavings in individual watertight containers beside your compost pile.
2. Layer 1 pail of kitchen waste, 1 pail of shavings and feces, 250 g to 1 kg of pet food and 2 pails worth of shredded paper.
3. Water the layers.
4. Cover the top of the pile with a thin layer of dirt.
5. Repeat steps 2, 3 and 4 when a new pail of kitchen scraps is available.
6. Use the aeration device to poke holes and add air to the pile every time you make a new set of layers.
7. A couple shovelfuls of compost will be ready to remove from the bottom of the pile in two to three months. Screen out any undigested feedstock and put it back at the top of the pile. The pile will continually produce more compost at the bottom every week until winter sets in.

Cookin' Hot Pile

- → 3 large garbage bags of elephant manure from the zoo or horse manure from the local equestrian centre
- → 3 large garbage bags of old wood chips or straw
- → 3 large garbage bags of rotting hay
- → water

Instructions:

1. Evenly mix manure, straw and hay with a compost fork and add water as needed.
2. Turn pile every three to four days.
3. Compost should be ready in two to three weeks.

Winter Composting

Composting can be slow and unproductive during cold Canadian winters. Thankfully, your plants don't grow in winter either, so yard waste and maintenance is pretty much a non-issue. Most people who want to compost in winter are dealing with the remnants of autumn cleanup or want to continue composting kitchen wastes year-round. One option is to take your compost bin indoors to a heated garage or basement. Worm bins, anaerobic enclosed bins and certain commercial automatic aerobic bins all successfully produce compost indoors. However, if you prefer to leave your rotting waste outside, you can still succeed at hot or cold winter composting.

Hot Winter Composting

Hot winter composting is worthwhile if you have a lot of yard waste from autumn cleanup and you want to deal with it right away so the finished product is ready for application in spring.

The first step for successful winter composting is to situate a single-unit compost bin in a convenient location close to your back door where your tramping feet won't damage dormant plants under the insulating snow. The location should also get plenty of warm winter sun.

Next, you need to insulate your bin from the cold. Left exposed to the air, your pile will cool off quickly, reducing or halting the speed of production.

Try hot winter composting if you have a lot of yard waste in autumn.

Rotating units and three-unit bins are difficult to insulate, so use a single-unit for the most success. You can insulate your bin with autumn leaves packed around the pile at least 45 cm deep. Stacking hay or straw bales around and over the pile also works well. If you want the pile to look tidy, purchase cut-to-shape, 7.5 cm thick styrofoam sheets to pack around and on top of your bin.

After you've insulated your bin, start building the compost pile right away, before the weather gets too cold. It should be at least 1.2 m³ of mixed, shredded or chopped browns and greens. Use a little warm water to make sure your dry materials are slightly moist as you build the pile. Do not water the pile after you finish building it because water will make it lose heat. Also, build your pile using a high nitrogen activator, such as manure, to make the pile heat up right away.

Use a compost thermometer to monitor the temperature. If the core of the pile starts to cool down significantly, turn the pile. Try not to turn the pile often (at maximum every 10 days) so it stays insulated and warm. Turning exposes the hot core of the pile to winter air, and it will lose heat. Leaving the compost pile unturned is okay, too.

To keep the pile warm, insert hot water bottles into the core of the pile.

Try cold winter composting to take care of your kitchen scraps.

You can also purchase an electric immersion heater (like a bird bath heater) and place it in a sealed jug of water in the middle of your bin to maintain a steady temperature throughout the winter. Keep the setting low for this option because you need to let the decomposers cycle through their life stages.

When the compost is ready, leave it in the insulated composter unit until you are ready to use it in spring.

Cold Winter Composting

Decomposers called psychrophiles happily live and reproduce in cold temperatures (-10° to 20° C). These are the decomposers that spoil the milk in your fridge if you leave it past the expiry date. If you want to compost your kitchen wastes in winter, just let psychrophiles do the work. They are slower than their warmer-weather cousins but will break down kitchen wastes in time for spring planting season.

As with winter hot composting, you must place your pile in a convenient, sunny location and insulate it so the temperature does not drop below -10° C.

Keep a container of shredded leaves next to the bin, and every time you empty your kitchen wastes in to the bin, cover them with a layer of leaves and maybe a sprinkling of dirt, if you have some. Flies and smells are not a huge concern in winter, so don't worry too much about thoroughly burying the wastes unless you have pests in the area.

By spring, at least half the wastes should have turned to finished compost. Once the pile thaws out, stir it to add air.

The rest of the matter will break down very quickly (within a week or two).

Cold Compost Storage

If you have a problem with rodents or pests in your area, you may want to consider cold compost storage. When you insulate your pile and keep it warmer than everywhere else outdoors, mice and other little critters will want to build a nest in it. This may not bother you because at least they are not nesting in your house or garage. However, you probably don't want their populations to grow and don't want to deal with ejecting them from their home in spring.

Cold compost storage involves thoroughly soaking your compost pile right before winter sets in. It will turn into a big Popsicle. Pests like warm, dry homes, so they will keep away from this icy monstrosity. Come spring, the pile will thaw out and you can mix in some dry materials to absorb the excess moisture. The freeze-thaw cycle helps weaken plant cells and makes decomposition super quick.

Cold compost storage can also involve storing kitchen wastes through winter. Keep a garbage can (or two) with a lid outside your back door. Dump your kitchen wastes into the can so they stay frozen over the winter months. In spring, empty the can, breaking up the frozen contents with a shovel, and build a hot compost pile, layering the frozen kitchen waste with dry materials saved from autumn cleanup. The waste should break down quickly once it has completely thawed.

Troubleshooting

There is no such thing as a perfect compost pile. Maintaining perfect air and moisture levels, biodiversity and temperatures are pretty much impossible to do even for composting professionals. For this reason, most of us are willing to settle for a functional bin that does not make us to work harder than we have to.

The first and best way to ensure your pile does what it should is to construct it with the right balance of greens and browns, and then add enough water, dirt and air. Once decomposition starts and the materials start to break down, the conditions in the bin may start to change, necessitating some intervention on your part to maintain the health of the pile. Keep an eye out for symptoms that indicate developing problems so you can take the necessary steps to improve the health of the pile.

Pile Smells Like Ammonia

The most common reason for a pile to smell like ammonia is that too much fresh, green waste, such as kitchen scraps or grass clippings, have been piled all at once without mixing them with enough dry, brown materials (should be equal weight; therefore, the volume of dry material may be up to double the volume of wet material). The solution is to mix more dry, brown material (such as autumn leaves) into your pile.

Another reason your pile might smell like ammonia is if the pile has turned anaerobic. The pile may have settled and compressed out the air, or it may have too much water. Either way, mix up the pile to get air inside and to expose excess water to the air so it can evaporate. Add bulky roughage, such as straw or whole leaves, to make sure air voids are maintained and excess moisture is absorbed.

If you are using an alkaline additive such as limestone powder (also known as calcium carbonate) to adjust the pH, it will chemically react with nitrogen in your pile, forming ammonia. Consider cutting back on how much of these additives you use, or wait until the compost is finished before you use them.

Pile Smells Putrid

Putrid smells are a by-product of anaerobic composting. Methane and ammonia combine to put off an unpleasant stench. To fix this problem, mix the pile to reintroduce air and kill off the anaerobes. A pile that is too wet can turn anaerobic. If you suspect this is the case, make sure your pile is in a well-drained area and has a lid to protect it against excess rain. Consider adding dry, brown material to absorb some of the excess moisture.

Pile Smells Rancid

If you put in eggs, meat, fats or milk products, you are almost guaranteed to have some bad smells (and flies and pests). If you insist on putting these items into your composter, bury them at least 15 cm under the surface of the pile.

Green, Goopy Sludge

If your pile turns into green goop, you probably have too much green waste. If you attempt to compost grass clippings on their own or mix them with kitchen wastes and other green wastes, you will likely get a goopy mess. Add brown materials to balance out the pile.

Pile Doesn't Heat Up

Not all piles need to heat up, but if you are trying to do hot composting and nothing is happening, there could be several reasons. The most common problem is that there is not enough high-nitrogen material in the pile.

Consider adding an organic activator such as poultry manure or cheap dog food to the middle of the pile.

Another reason could be inappropriate moisture levels. A dry pile will not heat up, so mix in some water until it is just moist. However, excess water can also prevent your pile from heating up. If the weather in your area is cool and wet, situate the pile in a hot, sunny location to dry it out a little.

Often a pile will not heat up if it is too small. The pile must be big enough (at least 1.2 m³) to insulate the core so it can stay hot after the initial rise in temperature.

Too much green waste, including grass clippings, can cause problems.

Cool external temperatures can also keep a pile from heating up. Most home compost piles are not able to heat up in winter. Consider further insulating your pile or moving it to a sunny location. Over turning your pile in cool, autumn temperatures can contribute to heat loss.

The last reason the pile might not be heating up is bioavailability. If the majority of your browns are big chunks of high-lignin materials, such as new wood chips or newspaper, the first decomposers will not be able to digest those foods easily. Consider mixing in an alternative source of browns, such as shredded autumn leaves, and some high-nitrogen manure to get the process started.

Pile Is Too Hot

This is an uncommon problem for backyard bins. The pile is too hot if it goes above 70° C, the temperature at which most decomposers start to die. Check the temperature of your pile with a compost thermometer, and turn it if it is too hot. The act of turning releases heat from the core. Watering can also lower the temperature, but be careful not to overwater the pile.

Pile Spontaneously Combusts

Yes, it is possible (though rare) for a pile to catch fire. The best way to prevent a compost fire is to keep the pile moist. Even a cold compost pile should be checked every week or two to make sure the contents don't dry out. Dry paper and straw lying on top of a hot pile in the sun or in a black, heat-absorbing compost bin can lead to a small fire. If you don't plan to water during the dry, hot summer months, consider keeping the pile in the shade so it doesn't dry out, or keep a lid on it to prevent excess evaporation.

Problem Pests

See Appendix A (p. 149)

Too much newspaper could prevent your pile from heating up.

On-Site Composting

If you are not a big fan of manual labour, on-site composting might be the best option for you. On-site composting does involve some aerobic and anaerobic microorganism activity, but most of the work is done by larger critters, such as worms and beetles. You don't have to put any effort into turning or structuring the pile for aeration. Your finished compost product is absorbed into the soil where it was started and is not intended as a batch to be spread around the garden as a top-dressing or used in a potting mix. There are a few different ways to do on-site composting: grass-cycling, mulching, sheet composting, comforter composting and stow and grow piles. As the name implies, you do not need a bin for on-site composting because you compost wastes directly on the site where you will use the finished product, saving you the effort of hauling waste and compost back and forth from the garden. However, the lack of bin means that only garden waste can be used—kitchen scraps are unsightly and attract pests if used for on-site composting.

Grasscycling

Often referred to as mulching, grass-cycling is the easiest and most efficient way to deal with grass clippings. Grasscycling allows you to water less often, forget about bagging grass and save money on fertilizer. All you have to do is mow with a mulching lawn mower and leave your grass clippings on the lawn.

If you don't have a mulching mower, you can use a regular mower without the bag attachment, though you may have to rake a little to break up any clumps or windrows of clippings on the lawn. You could also retrofit your old lawn mower with a converter kit to block the grass from shooting out the side of the mower. The mulching mower and retrofit cover ensure that clippings are double cut by the blades before being evenly deposited over the grass. Your lawn's health will improve and you will save time and energy not having to bag all that grass for garbage collection.

When you leave the clippings on the lawn, they work their way down to the soil level, where they quickly break down into the soil. All the nutrients that were drawn from the soil by the growing grass return to feed new growth, which reduces your need for fertilizers. Also, grass is 90 percent water. When the grass breaks down, it waters the soil; therefore, you don't need to water as often. Watering once a week is sufficient as long as you water deeply (at least 2.5 cm of applied water). Water in the evening or early morning so that water is not wasted through evaporation.

To successfully grasscycle, keep your lawn mower blades sharp and set high (6 to 7.5 cm). Cut the grass regularly so that the clippings do not get too long; they should be small enough to settle near the roots of your grass. Cut the grass twice a week on hot summer days and switch to once a week as summer cools off. The clippings will not be noticeable or unsightly and will completely disappear after two to three days as long as they are spread evenly over the lawn (not in windrows or clumps). To prevent windrows and clumps, mow the lawn only when it is dry. Cutting a wet lawn damages it and dulls the blades on your mower.

Grasscycling is beneficial to your lawn, so leave the bag off the mower.

Some myths have popped up over the years about grasscycling and the onset of thatch. Contrary to popular fears, grasscycling does not contribute to thatch. Thatch is a root problem that happens when the soil and roots are overwatered, overfertilized or deprived of oxygen. Overfertilization causes the roots to grow too fast with no room to expand. The roots begin to move above the soil level, where they dry out and die. The roots and stems break down slowly because they are resistant to decomposition. Also, if bacteria in the soil are starved of oxygen from compression of the soil and overwatering, they cannot quickly break down the thatch. Pesticide and herbicide use can also contribute to thatch in that it may kill the bacteria responsible for breaking down the thatch. If you have thatch problems, rent an aerator machine to add air to the soil and give roots room to grow. Consider raking in a thin layer of compost evenly over the grass and aeration holes to reintroduce the microorganisms responsible for breaking down the thatch.

Grasscycling

- Saves time and energy because you don't have to bag clippings
- Is easy to do
- Reduces the need for fertilization
- Reduces watering
- Saves landfill space
- Requires regular mower blade sharpening
- Requires frequent mowing

The thatch layer is between the white lines.

Mulching

You can also use your grass clippings as mulch around the base of your plants and in the rows of your garden to suppress weeds, retain moisture and prevent erosion. Layer the mulch 4 to 8 cm thick around the base of your plants or on exposed soil in your garden. If you feel like being innovative, use newspaper (8 to 10 sheets thick), cardboard or rhubarb leaves as an organic landscaping fabric underneath your mulch of choice. Rhubarb leaves are especially great at preventing weed growth because they are toxic to most plants and insects and will discourage ants and slugs from making a home in your garden.

Mulches such as shredded yard wastes, straw, leaves and grass clippings are cheap alternatives to purchased wood or bark chips and will break down every year or so, enriching your soil for the next year. Natural mulches also attract worms and beetles that work to improve your soil. Kitchen scraps are not ideal for mulch because you want to keep your garden aesthetically pleasing with a uniform mulch cover and not attract pests.

Mulching

- Suppresses weeds
- Retains soil moisture
- Puts some nutrients back in the soil as it breaks down
- Is aesthetically pleasing
- Saves money on purchased mulches
- Is an easy way to deal with grass clippings
- Is an easy way to deal with leaves in autumn
- Needs replacing every year or so

Straw is a cheap mulch that will enrich your soil.

Sheet Composting

Sheet composting is similar to mulching. Spread a thin layer (2.5 to 5 cm thick) of leaves, yard waste or grass clippings over an entire garden plot and use a rototiller to till it under the soil. This can also be done with a live cover crop that you don't plan to use, such as unseeded weeds, clover, alfalfa, winter peas, mustard or fenugreek. Legumes are often the cover crop of choice because the bacteria near their roots fix nitrogen into the soil. Sheet composting with a live crop is called green manure and is typically done in large-scale agriculture. This type of composting is slow and can take the garden out of service for up to one season. Some people like to leave the thin layer of yard waste to decompose on top of the soil instead of tilling it in. Others till it under and add a mulch layer on top of the soil to protect it from weed growth and to retain the moisture that is essential to decomposition.

Sheet Composting
- Is done on a large scale
- Is slow
- Usually requires a rototiller or tilling machinery

Any plant in the Fabaceae family can be used as a live cover crop.

Comforter Composting

In their book *The Complete Compost Gardening Guide*, Barbara Pleasant and Deborah Martin share the technique of comforter composting. Comforter composting is similar to sheet composting but requires no tilling and slightly larger mounds of decomposing materials. The idea is to put yard waste in a short (30 cm) but broad pile that will break down over the course of a season. Make a comforter compost bed in a location that is easily accessible as you work so you can throw your yard debris in it as you go. Choose a spot where you want a new garden bed or that needs some new soil. Without bothering to clear the area of existing plants or grass, start layering fresh waste, dead waste and soil. Water often but don't bother mixing. Next year, you will have a new, fertile garden bed to plant in. If you do not want to see your pile in the middle of your garden, cover it with a layer of finished compost or topsoil as you go and plant around it. The nutrients from the decomposing pile will leach into the surrounding area, feeding the nearby plants.

If your area is infected with slugs, they will be attracted to the pile. This is a good thing because they will be eating the compostable materials instead of your garden plants, but you should set some beer-bowl traps in the pile to kill them off. If you do not kill them, they will multiply in number and make your slug problem worse.

Comforter Composting

- Is easy
- Involves no turning or aerating
- Builds a new growing area
- Is slow (takes one year)
- Can attract slugs

Comforter composting will create a new, fertile garden bed.

Stow and Grow Pile

Also known as a lasagne composter, grow heap or hidden composter, the stow and grow pile is an active, on-site compost pile that requires no turning or active work. You build it as a batch and plant in it so that it is hidden once the plants begin to grow. As with comforter composting, it should be no more than 30 cm high, but it can cover a large surface area.

The stow and grow pile can be started even in the worst parts of your garden where acidic conditions make growing anything difficult. Just lay down a layer of wet newspaper and a few layers of brown matter, green materials and topsoil. The topsoil is important and is required in a higher quantity than in a traditional compost pile because it provides plant roots with structure and a place for stable growth. Build the pile in autumn during cleanup, and it will be ready for planting in spring, even though it will be only partially decomposed after winter. Plant some hardy legume or vegetable seeds in the pile. You can experiment with different types of pumpkin, squash or even raspberry seeds to see which varieties grow best in the active pile. Be warned that not all plants are comfortable growing in a live compost heap, and it may take a bit of trial and error to find the right crop. Some people have had more success by putting a pile of twigs or brush in a channel under the layers to make the pile into a mound with great drainage.

Stow and Grow Pile

- Is easy
- Is hidden
- Is a batch system
- No turning is required
- Is not intended for growing all plant types

Try growing squash in your active stow and grow pile.

Troubleshooting

Maintaining your on-site compost pile should be relatively simple in comparison to other composting methods—you are relying on nature to do its thing in its own time. Because you are not doing hot compost or using kitchen wastes, you don't have to worry about many of the troubles you would find with other forms of composting.

Grasscycling Troubles

Dry Grass on the Lawn

You will find dry grass on your lawn only if you don't break up windrows and clumps of grass. Don't mow the grass when it's wet, or the clippings will clump. If you have an old mower without a mulching attachment, rake apart clumps so the grass is evenly spread over the lawn. Also, if the grass is too long (usually the first cut of the growing season) the clippings will sit on top of the grass. Consider bagging and composting the first clippings of the season and grasscycling everything after that.

Mulching and Comforter Composting Troubles

Comforter Compost is not Breaking Down

It can take one to two years to decompose a pile on its own. Decomposers such as worms and beetles can target a pile and break it down in as little as four months. If you are not satisfied with the progress of your pile, water it enough to keep it moist so the decomposers will stick around. Make sure feedstocks are chopped up—the smaller they are, the faster they break down.

Slugs

See Appendix A (p. 149)

> Confess yourself to heaven,
> Repent what's past, avoid what is to come,
> And do not spread the compost on the weeds
> To make them ranker.
>
> —Shakespeare, *Hamlet*

Successful Anaerobic Composting Methods

Anaerobic composting is the decomposition of wastes through fermentation, which results in the production of humic acids, humus and gases. If an aerobic composting environment should be like a forest floor, an anaerobic composting environment should be like a rotting bog. Water, plenty of fresh, green wastes, and the rich smell of decay add up to moist, rich humus that can be used around your garden.

There are a few advantages and disadvantages to anaerobic composting. This form of composting can be used to reduce waste or improve the soil where it is situated. It is a cold composting method that preserves nitrogen in the pile that would normally be lost in the oxidation of a hot compost pile. However, it can be smelly and attract animals unless it is protected.

Because anaerobic bacteria thrive without air, anaerobic composting units are often situated underground or in airtight containers. There are three main types of anaerobic composting units: sealed, trench and pit composters. Some people may argue that all but the sealed composters fall into the aeration composter category; however, although the piles often start off fluffy and full of air, they usually end up at least partly anaerobic because they aren't turned.

Sealed Anaerobic Composters

Totally Enclosed Units

If you have limited space and want to reduce waste, there are a few easy ways to make finished compost in an airtight compost unit on your balcony or in your home. Fill a sealed garbage can, a black plastic garbage bag (doubled is safest) or a bucket with a lid with one-third kitchen scraps, one-third dirt and one-third garden waste, then add water until the mixture is moist. The anaerobes cannot easily break down wood lignin, so do not use paper, wood chips or sawdust as a brown, carbonaceous material in your bin. This is a batch system, so save up your wastes, fill up the bag or

You can use plastic garbage bags for anaerobic composting.

bin and don't open it until you are certain it is done, or you will get a waft of putrid smells. Let it sit in the sun and roll it around every week or so, and you should have finished compost in two to six months. The resulting compost will be very moist and should be aired out for a few weeks before it is screened and used in the garden.

Drainage Units

You can also successfully compost high-nitrogen waste, such as kitchen scraps including meats, bones, milk products and eggs, without adding any carbonaceous material. Dig a hole 15 to 30 cm deep, and partly bury a bottomless bucket in the hole. Fill it as full as you can with your kitchen scraps, close the lid and do not open it for three to six months. It helps to have two or more buckets and to rotate back and forth between them as you fill them. If you have a large volume of high-nitrogen materials, use a barrel instead of a bucket. You can fill the barrel gradually, but open the lid no more than twice a week so you don't kill the anaerobes.

If you don't have a barrel, make a big pile of nitrogen wastes and cover it tightly with thick, impermeable plastic cloth or a tarp, using bricks or cement blocks to hold the tarp in place. You do not need to mix the pile and should not take the tarp off other than for watering once a month. If you fail to seal the tarp tightly over the pile, you risk attracting pests and releasing bad smells.

In this high-nitrogen method of anaerobic composting, you need to design your pile, bucket or barrel for drainage, or the resulting product will be a wet sludge instead of dark, crumbly dirt. Though this form of composting can handle meats, it is not good to add fatty waste, which can slow down the composting process considerably. Bones decompose but may need to be screened through several batches before they break down. Dry carbonaceous material, such as leaves, paper, straw, etc., are best kept out of this type of compost bin and should be composted aerobically instead. The carbonaceous material will dry out the pile and likely slow the composting process.

Use anaerobic methods to successfully compost high-nitrogen waste.

How to Build a Barrel Drainage Composter

1. Cut the bottom off of a bucket.

2. Dig a hole 15–30 cm deep and line the bottom of the hole with hardware cloth.

3. Put the bucket in the hole and fill it full with your kitchen scraps

4. Put the lid on the bucket and do not open it for 3–6 months.

If you have pests in your area, use a hard plastic or metal bucket and line the bottom of the hole and bucket with hardware cloth to prevent animals from accessing the contents of the bin. Make sure the mesh has wide enough holes to allow worms and other small decomposers access to your pile from below.

See the facing page for plans to construct your own bin, or see the Anaerobic Composter Units Available for Purchase section (p. 102) for reviews of some of the commercial models available.

Sealed Anaerobic Composters

- Are batch compost systems
- Smell foul if opened early
- Can be made from cheap supplies
- Protect against pests when in solid, sealed or lined containers
- Can result in sludgy compost
- Can digest meat, bones, eggs and milk products

Trench Composting

Trench composting involves digging a row at least 30 cm deep into the soil, spreading an even, shallow mix of finely chopped yard wastes in the trench, and then burying it with the original soil.

This method is good in a garden where you can set up a rotating planting system. Plant a row of seeds beside which you build your trench compost row, and next to that make a walking path. The following year, rotate the rows—plant seeds where the trench was, dig a new trench on the old walking path and walk where the seeds were in the previous year. This method is similar to on-site composting; however, the bacteria will not get air as the waste decomposes, and the trench often turns anaerobic.

Leave weeds out when trench composting.

If a garden require it, now trench it ye may,
one trench not a yard, from another go lay;
which being well filled with muck by and by,
to cover with mould, for a season to lie.

–Thomas Tusser

Trench composting still requires an even mix of green and brown materials, either combined or in shallow layers. Cutting up the waste is important because it ensures that everything will break down by the following year. Adding weeds to this system is a bad idea, especially if they are seeding.

The compost decomposers and the plants in the neighbouring row may compete for the nitrogen in the soil. Use a high-nitrogen organic fertilizer in your seed row, or make the rows far enough apart to prevent nitrogen loss from the soil around your growing plants. If you have a problem with pests such as raccoons, rats or dogs, consider using only yard waste and not putting in kitchen scraps. You could also lay a few narrow sheets of plywood over the trench, or stake down some chicken wire or hardware cloth to prevent big pests from digging it up.

Trench Composting

- Is a gradual process (six months to one year)
- Does not need to be turned
- Requires finely chopped wastes
- Should contain only yard wastes if pets or pests are a concern
- Seeded weeds should not be included

Rotate the location of the trench from year to year (left).
Use only yard waste in your trench if you have pests in your area (below).

Pit Composting

The pit composter is rather like a latrine or outhouse for your kitchen waste. You can use the pit year-round because its underground location insulates it from cold winter weather. Find a spot in your yard that is elevated and easy to access but that is not subject to flooding or near a groundwater source. Dig a hole 60 to 90 cm deep, avoiding underground gas lines and tree root systems. Throw in your kitchen wastes and eventually cover up the last 30 cm with soil or compost. The pit composter is not a batch unit and can handle everyday wastes from your kitchen. You can even throw in meats, bones, milk products, breads and seeded weeds (keep the weeds at least 30 cm below the surface of the soil to prevent them from germinating). Although this type of composter can handle small quantities of green yard waste, large volumes of leaves and grass would be better composted in an aerobic unit.

As the waste breaks down, it liquefies and adds nutrients to the

You can use an old door to cover your composting pit.

surrounding soil. Therefore, situating your pit in an area with good drainage that does not fill with water during rainy weather is important. The volume of the waste will reduce quickly, and you can expect the hole not to fill with solids for a really long time. You cannot use the finished compost from a pit other than to plant over it when it is full and covered over.

Because this is an anaerobic pit, you need to protect it from pests and prevent it from smelling foul. Cover the hole with a heavy, airtight lid that you can secure in place. A latch will prevent animals from lifting up the lid. The cover must be strong enough to support the weight of a person who accidentally stands on it. A sheet of wood 2.5 to 5 cm thick, like the kind you would see on an old well, will suffice. You could also retrofit an old door to cover the hole for a more pleasing appearance.

If you have rats or mice in your area, consider lining the hole with hardware cloth or steel mesh so the pests can't dig through to the pile. Bury a bottomless plastic barrel with a lid to prevent burrowers from accessing the pile. Try not to open the lid more than twice per week, or you risk letting in too much air and killing the anaerobes. Store your waste in a kitchen catcher, and empty it every few days into the composter.

Water the pile frequently to prevent flies and nasty smells. If the pile dries out, the bacteria will die, and the composting process will halt. If your pit has proper drainage, water as often as you like. Anaerobes thrive in a watery environment without air, so extra water is better than not enough. Have a tub of soil or finished compost on hand so you can throw a little on top of fresh waste to keep smells down and to reduce the number of flies.

Some people like to put a perforated pipe in the middle of the pit to encourage aerobic composting, or at least to reduce smells. Other people have been successful at aeration composting in a pit composter; however, it does require getting into the hole for turning. In this case, make the hole no more than 45 cm deep so you don't strain your back turning it.

Pit Composting
- Composts almost all kitchen wastes (except fats)
- Is easy
- Requires initial effort to dig a deep hole
- May attract pests unless adequately protected
- May emit foul odours unless properly sealed
- Must be in an easily accessible location
- Has no finished product other than rich soil on location
- Is not intended for yard wastes

Anaerobic Composter Units Available for Purchase

If you don't want to make your own anaerobic composting unit, there are several units available for purchase at hardware stores.

The Green Cone

One of the most popular anaerobic pit composting units is the Green Cone. The sole purpose of this unit and other anaerobic composting units like it is to reduce waste. Not everyone has the luxury of throwing organic wastes into a landfill, so an anaerobic digester is an easy way to get rid of that waste.

The manufacturers of the cone claim that it is an aerobic unit with sun-absorbing action that circulates air around the cone. However, the bacteria act suspiciously like anaerobic bacteria: it cannot easily compost wood products with lignin, and the final product is a sludgy liquid.

The cone is half buried underground. There is no turning or aeration involved—you just throw in your kitchen scraps, some water and a bit of activator mix (it comes with the composter) and leave it. Designed in bear country in Ontario, the cone protects the food from all pests, and the lid keeps smells from escaping.

In the bin, the food liquefies into sludgy compost that leaches into the ground surrounding the bin. Every two to three years or so, the bin is moved to a new spot in the yard, and the old hole is covered (or the solids from the bottom basket can be dug out and buried elsewhere). The soil is now rich and fertile and can be planted on; however, this bin does not produce a finished product that can be spread around the yard like regular compost.

The Bokashi Compost Bucket

First started in Japan, this indoor/outdoor anaerobic trench composting method quickly decomposes wastes, and there is little effort involved. Just fill the special lidded bucket with kitchen wastes (including meat, eggs and milk products)

and sprinkle each deposit with the special EM (effective microorganism) inoculated Bokashi activator. The activator pickles the food, preventing smells and bugs. After two weeks, the bucket should be full. Drain off the compost tea to use on your plants, and empty the undigested pickled waste in a trench and bury it. The pickling ensures that the food breaks down faster than it would normally, so you can collect the finished compost and use it around your garden (or plant directly on top of it) after only two months.

The Bokashi Bucket is essentially a 40 L pail with a spigot at the bottom to drain off compost tea. It is a very popular compost bin in Australia and New Zealand, and it can be ordered online and shipped to Canada. Some retailers in Canada sell the Bokashi Bucket and inoculant, but not many, so you may have to look around for a local source. Another option is to make your own homemade Bokashi bucket and inoculants using the purchased products as a base (like making your own yeast).

Recipe for 1 L of Activated EM-1® Bacteria

→ 800 mL warm (38° C), dechlorinated water

→ 50 mL molasses

→ 50 mL EM-1®

Instructions:

1. Pour the water into a clean, airtight 1 L plastic bottle or container.

2. Add the molasses* and EM-1® to the bottle.

3. Shake the bottle to dissolve the molasses. Top off with water.

4. Cap the bottle tightly and keep it in a warm place.

5. When the pH of the solution has been at 3.7 or below for five to seven days, the Activated EM-1® is ready to use. Use within 30 to 45 days.

* Dissolve the molasses with warm or hot water before adding it to the bottle. As the microbes digest the sugars during fermentation, pressure builds in the container.

To prevent the container from rupturing, remove the lid so the pressure can be released, then reseal the container. You may have to go though this process one or more times per day.

Bokashi Activator Recipe

- → 30 mL EM-1°
- → 30 mL sugar cane molasses
- → 750 mL hot dechlorinated water (60° to 80° C)
- → 750 mL warm dechlorinated water (approx. 40° C)
- → 5 kg wheat bran or rice bran

Instructions:

1. Mix the molasses with the hot water, and stir in the warm water.

2. Add EM-1°.

3. Mix the liquid thoroughly into the bran.

4. Squeeze some of the bran into a ball. If it holds its shape and no extra liquid comes out, it has the correct level of moisture (35 to 40 percent). If it is too dry, add more water and EM-1°. Put the mixture into a bag or container.

5. If using a bag, tie it tightly, squeezing out excess air. If using a container, press down mixture and cover the container tightly.

6. Place mixture in a warm location where it will be out of the way. Let it ferment for at least two weeks.

When fermentation is complete, you may notice some white mould on or in the bokashi. This is good. However, black or green mould is not good and means air got into the container or the mixture was too moist.

You can use the bokashi as is, or dry it for long-term storage. Either way, store it in an airtight bag or container and use it within one year.

Troubleshooting

Anaerobic composting is not as popular as aerobic composting because there can be unpleasant results if the bin is mismanaged. However, anaerobic composting can be easy and painless and is a viable option for people with limited space who want to try composting indoors. As long as you take the proper preventative measures or manage problems before they get out of hand, you should not experience any unpleasant side effects from owning the bin.

Foul Smells

The reality of anaerobic composting is that it produces methane and ammonia as food decomposes. A healthy anaerobic pile smells like sulphur and other putrid smelling gases. If your pile smells all the time, your bin is not sealed properly. As long as you have a tight lid for your compost bucket or pile, the gasses and smells should stay contained in the bin. When you take finished compost out of a sealed container, the accumulated gases will escape all at once (which is okay). Let the finished compost dry out outside; the smells will quickly dissipate as the anaerobes die in the air.

Green, Sludgy Compost

If the final result of your anaerobic compost project is goopy sludge, you likely did not have enough drainage in your bin—especially if you used only high-nitrogen kitchen wastes. Move the bin to a location with better drainage. When using a fully sealed compost unit in your home that is not intended for drainage, use less nitrogen waste and add a balance of carbonaceous wastes and dirt so sludge doesn't form. This method takes longer than the other anaerobic methods but produces useable compost for your garden.

Slow Decomposition

A pile that is too dry or has too much wood waste decomposes slowly. A healthy anaerobic pile should have a slimy, goopy texture as it decomposes. Check the moisture level and add water if necessary.

Also, anaerobes cannot break down lignin in wood. Stop adding carbonaceous materials such as leaves, paper, straw or sawdust to get the anaerobes working. Make sure the pile is packed tight and that the lid stays on to prevent air from accessing the compost.

Problem Pests

Ants

See Appendix A (p. 149)

Fruit Flies

See Appendix A (p. 149)

Large Pests

If your area has a raccoon, opossum or other pest problem, use a hard plastic container and line the hole or pit with hardware cloth or metal mesh. If you trench compost, cover the top of the trench with a sheet of plywood or stake down hardware cloth and don't use kitchen scraps in your trench.

Opossum

Worm Composting

The Latin word for "worm" is *vermi* and is easy to remember because it kind of sounds like "wormy" with a German accent. "Vermicomposting" is the technical term for composting with worms. Vermicomposting is different from traditional composting in that it is primarily done indoors in an enclosed bin instead of a big pile out in the garden. This is great news if you live in an apartment complex, if you don't have access to a garden, if you are practicing a form of composting that does not use kitchen waste or if you are concerned about attracting large pests such as raccoons, skunks or bears to your yard, as you might with a traditional backyard compost bin. Vermicomposting is not a system designed to handle yard wastes, but it is an excellent way to process kitchen wastes into a great finished product for your plants.

Your New Pets

Worms are great pets. They are small, gentle and cute. And, they require little attention, with no walks, barking or fur to contend with. You can leave them for two weeks without arranging for a sitter and with the happy knowledge that they will not resent your absence or punish you by chewing on your favourite shoes (unless you put your shoes in the bin).

Having a worm bin is a great conversation starter—you can show the worms off to your friends without worrying about allergic reactions, and you can play the gracious host by supplying your friends with their own worms if they are interested in starting their own bin. Worms are cheap to set up, and they save you money: you don't have to buy them food, pay to dispose of your waste or buy fertilizer for your soil.

Your kids will really like worms because of the unique status of having an unusual pet. Kids are also fascinated by the worms' lifecycle, and you can use your worm bin as a tool for teaching your children about nature's cycle of life, death and renewal. The kids can investigate the egg sacks, pregnant worms, baby worms, adult worms and all the helper decomposers that coexist with the worms in your bin.

Getting Over the Creepy Crawlies

Many people, women in particular, have been socially trained to fear worms. Horror movies and TV shows often terrorize audiences with stories of

Worms are low maintenance pets that take care of your kitchen waste for you.

parasitic worms from outer space or mind-controlling tapeworms. Because of these socially contrived fears, earthworms have been unfairly lumped into the same category as some of their more dangerous cousins. However, there is nothing to fear from earthworms. They have no teeth and cannot eat anything that is not already dead and decaying. They rely on other decomposers to soften up their food before they eat it and therefore cannot eat any live plants or fresh waste. They do not carry diseases. In fact, they have more cause to fear us than we do them. If earthworms could tell tales, I'm sure they would have horror stories of their own about fishermen's hooks and children's feet after a rainstorm. The best way to lose our fear of worms is to understand them and approach them with the attitude that they are an integral part of nature.

Red wigglers like the humus layer of the forest floor.

Introducing the Red Wiggler

There are more than 4400 different species of earthworm; however, only a few species thrive in a worm compost bin. The most popular is *Eisenia fetida,* the red wiggler. It is called the red wiggler because of its dark red appearance and its tendency to flop around on a fishing hook.

This worm is native to the southern United States, where winters are warm.

The red wiggler does not like to burrow underground but instead prefers the moist environment of decaying matter on top of the soil. It lives in the humus layer where fallen leaves and other dead things break down. This worm reproduces quickly and is content living in close confines. With plenty of food on the forest floor to eat year-round, the red wiggler happily developed a voracious appetite.

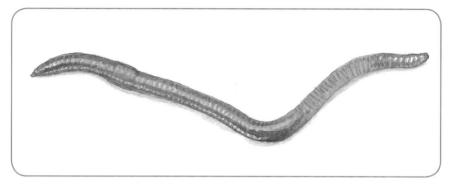

Eisenia fetida

Originally imported to Canada as fishing bait, the red wiggler swiftly earned a reputation for its efficient ability to break down waste. A composting bin is very similar to this worm's natural habitat. In your bin, the red wiggler does not need soil; instead, it makes its home in the scrap wastes you feed it. It is happy living confined and in large numbers in your bin; one bin alone can host thousands of worms.

The red wiggler worm has five hearts, two stomachs, one reproductive sack and one brain. It does not have eyes, ears, a nose or teeth. It has a red hemoglobin blood system similar to that of a human. Its digestive system is similar to that of a bird: it has a crop and a gizzard. Because the red wiggler has no teeth, it feeds on items that other decomposers have already softened or partly broken down. The food goes into the first stomach (the crop) and then makes its way to the gizzard, where the food is ground by small bits of grit, such as sand or eggshells. Finally, the food passes into the long intestine and out the worm's anus as worm castings (worm compost). You can see intestines and castings in a red wiggler through its translucent skin if you hold it up to the light.

The red wiggler breathes through its skin, which needs to stay moist at all times. It wanders blindly in the soil, using microscopic hairs called setae to grip the soil as it moves. It has only one defensive mechanism: when threatened, it emits a yellow, lubricating liquid that allows it to slip out of the jaws of a predator. The liquid also has a foul smell to persuade potential predators that the worm is not a tasty treat.

The best survival strategy of the species is its fast reproductive rate. This worm is a hermaphrodite, making the mating process simple and efficient. It takes the red wiggler 8 to 10 weeks from the time of its birth to reach adulthood. To reproduce, it seeks out another adult worm, identifiable by the fully developed reproductive organ, called a clitellum, visible as a thick band close to the worm's head. The two worms become attached using sticky mucus emitted from their clitellums. After mating, each

L. rubellus can survive being transferred to the garden.

worm secretes a liquid from its clitellum that hardens around the clitellum, forming a cocoon that the adult worm pushes off its body. As the worm backs out of the cocoon, the cocoon passes over the fertilized ovaries, collecting the developing eggs and sperm. It takes three to four days for the worm to completely free itself from the cocoon. The cocoon releases up to 10 baby worms within three weeks. A healthy adult worm will live for one to two years and can produce two to three cocoons every week for six months to one year.

As you can imagine, in less than one month, a handful of worms will reproduce into a whole bin full. However, don't worry that you will have an uncontrollable population of worms bursting out of your bin. A worm population will stabilize once it has reached the number

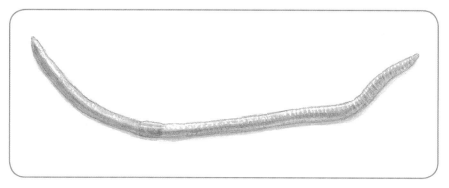

Lumbricus rubellus

that is sustainable by the food available in the bin and the space provided.

Other Composting Worm Species

Eisenia fetida is not the only worm suitable for a compost bin. *E. andrei* is similar in appearance, shares the same eating and living habits and happily co-exists with *E. fetida*. Another good composting worm is *Lumbricus rubellus,* otherwise known as the red worm or dung worm. It is good for composting large amounts of manure and for commercial composting. *L. rubellus* is versatile in that it can live in compost bins or the soil and may be one of the few composting worms that can survive being transferred to the garden when your worm bin is ready to harvest. *Perionyx excavatus* (the Indian blue worm) and *Eudrilus eugeniae* (the African nightcrawler) are warm-climate composting worms that have a delicate constitution and like to escape their bins. However, they compost efficiently as long as you have a warm place to keep them and a tightly lidded bin.

The worms you find in your garden or lawn (commonly known as nightcrawlers, earth workers or rain worms) should not be used in a worm bin. They are not as effective in processing waste because they are not happy living in large numbers in a shallow bin without soil. As well, these Canadian earthworm species are not efficient composters because they are content to live with less food than their southern cousins. Canadian worms have developed the instinct to burrow deep below the frost layer of the soil to survive cold winters. Winter kills many worms every year, so they are used to living in small numbers and prefer to have the freedom to spread out across the garden or yard. During winter months, their diet is sparse and they can survive on very little food. When held in a shallow bin, Canadian worms are unhappy, and no matter how much food you give them, they will never be able to consume as much as the red wiggler. The bin will start to smell because the worms will not process the food before it begins to decompose anaerobically.

Worm Care

Before starting your own worm bin, consider the environment you will place your worms in. Composting worms enjoy the same temperatures as humans. An appropriate temperature range for the storage of their bin is 10° to 30° C; they cannot survive in a bin that is placed in below 0° C temperatures for more than an hour or two. They also prefer not to be left in a bin that the hot summer sun has turned into an oven. Bins can be stored on a balcony over summer, but they

You can keep your worm bin on your balcony in summer.

must be in a shaded spot where they will not get too hot. Many homeowners store their worm bins outside over the warm months of the year and put them in the basement or heated garage over winter. Make sure your bin is accessible so you remember to check it and feed the worms regularly.

Creating a Habitat for Healthy Worms

Most creatures need four basic things to survive: air, water, food and shelter. You must provide your worms with these basic elements for them to survive in their bin. Despite the copious amounts of information provided below, making a worm bin is actually fairly painless. Just follow the six steps and your bin will be ready for you to add your new worms.

Step 1: Choosing a bin

To build a successful worm habitat, you first need to provide shelter for your worms in the form of a worm bin. The bin must be resistant to decay, preferably watertight and built with aeration in mind. Substances that are resistant to decay include glass, metal, plastic and wood—though wood will break down after a few years and metal is subject to rust. Cardboard boxes are not good worm bins because the moisture from the bin will swiftly seep into the structure, the worms will begin eating the walls and the box will quickly decay or at least fall apart when moved.

Glass: Some people have successfully converted an old 20 L aquarium into a worm house. The shape and watertight nature of an aquarium are well suited to vermicomposting. Reusing an aquarium is a great way to cut down the cost of purchasing or making a bin, and it keeps the old aquarium out of the landfill. Keep in mind that the narrow shape of the aquarium is not great for putting in large amounts of food, and the aquarium's depth may cause compaction as the bedding and food settle—possibly causing anaerobic conditions and smells.

Glass is a difficult medium to use if you plan to construct your own bin. You may need special glass-cutting equipment to size the sheets and make air holes. A glass bin is also heavy, especially when full of bedding and food.

Although glass bins are transparent, allowing you to see the decomposition process as it happens (which could be especially interesting for children), worms are not fond of light and—unlike ants in an ant farm—will mostly stay away from the outer edges of the bin unless it is stored in a dark location. You will likely just see the decomposing food if you keep the bin out in a well lit area.

Metal: Not many people use metal worm bins. They can be very heavy and can have sharp edges that could cause injury. Also, they tend to rust because of the moisture in the bin. However, if the bin is replaced before rust becomes a serious issue, a metal bin is just as

suitable as any other. Metal bins are probably not as popular as other types because there are few suitable containers available on the market, and not many people know how to construct a homemade bin of metal. You could use a garbage can that you fill half full of bedding, but you risk compaction and anaerobic conditions if you let the can get too full. If you have metallurgy skills or a friend who is a welder, you could easily arrange for the construction of an appropriately sized bin.

Wood: Wood is very popular worm bin material because it "breathes." It absorbs excess moisture and acts as a wick to balance out humidity in the bin. Few manufactured wooden bins are available on the market; however, you can easily construct a bin of any shape or size. Wood, construction tools and know-how are readily available to the layman woodworker.

The breathable nature of wood leaves it vulnerable to decay. A wooden worm bin will last only two to three years before it needs to be replaced. When it leaks profusely or cannot hold its shape and the walls start to separate from each other, it is time to look for a new bin. Wood can be heavy, depending on the thickness of the sheets you use. Be sure to use untreated plywood or lumber; chemicals from treated wood and particleboard can seep into your bin and kill your worms.

Plastic: Plastic is a very popular medium for worm bins because there are many inexpensive commercial tubs and bins available from most home supply stores. You can convert a plastic tub designed for storage into a worm bin. Standard 60 x 45 x 30 cm storage bins are waterproof, lightweight and come with tight-fitting lids and handles, making them easy to move. Cut holes into the lid or sides of the bin for aeration, or even put a spout at the bottom to drain excess moisture.

Once you've chosen what material you want your bin to be made of, you must decide what size and shape would best suit your needs. It should be large enough to accommodate the food waste you put in. Over the course of a week, measure or estimate the amount of kitchen waste that you produce. For every 500 g waste, you need 30 cm² of surface area in your bin. For example, if you produce 1.5 kg of waste per week,

you will need a bin that is 90 cm² at the bottom.

The depth of your bin should not exceed 60 cm and is best kept at 30 to 45 cm to prevent compaction and loss of air spaces.

Step 2: Providing air

Worms need air to breathe, and so do all their helpful decomposer buddies that share the bin. To avoid killing your worms and having a foul-smelling, anaerobic bin, make sure your bin has air holes in the lid and/or on the sides. A lid is not essential, but without one, you risk drying out your bin and exposing it to flies and pests.

The best way to protect your bin from fruit flies and other pesky critters is to tape plastic window screening with

Make sure your bin has air holes.

the smallest grid you can find over the air holes. Often, even the smallest screening is not small enough to keep out the tiny flies, so experiment with doubling and offsetting the screen to prevent flies from sneaking through it.

Step 3: Gathering your bedding

Once you have selected the right bin, you need to provide your worms with bedding to move around in. Think of bedding as furniture for your worms' new home. Bedding is important because it absorbs moisture from decomposing waste, shelters the worms from the sun, protects the waste from flies and keeps the bin from smelling bad.

The best bedding is readily available, dead, brown, high-carbon material. You can use shredded newspaper, office paper or cardboard, dried grass, straw, brown leaves, wood chips, finished compost or partly composted manure. Newspaper and office paper are easy to come by if you live in the city. Manure compost and straw are easy to find if you live on a farm or an acreage. Leaves are accessible to almost everyone in autumn.

Step 4: Providing moisture

Water is important for any compost bin, but it is especially so in a worm bin. Worms breathe through their skin. When a worm's skin is wet, it acts as a membrane that transfers air in and out of the worm's body. However, this does not mean that worms can breathe underwater. They need an environment that is damp but not sopping wet, or they

Gather your bedding before you acquire any worms.

will drown. You've probably seen worms crawling onto sidewalks when it rains to avoid drowning in the waterlogged soil; if you let your bin get too wet, you will see them crawling up the sides of your bin to avoid the same fate. The ideal dampness is similar to that of a wrung-out sponge. If you wet and then squeeze out a sponge, you can see the glistening of moisture on it, but no water drips out. The same should be true for the bedding you use in your bin. Add enough water to make the bedding damp but not so much that you get a puddle of water at the bottom of your bin.

For dry bedding such as paper, leaves, wood chips and straw, the best way to add the right amount of water is to soak the bedding and then wring it out. Get a bucket, tub or plastic bag that won't

leak. Fill the container with your bedding, and then add water until the bedding is fully immersed and soaking wet. In handfuls, begin to remove the wet bedding from the watery container, wringing it as dry as you can or shaking off excess water until it no longer drips. Transfer the damp bedding to the worm bin.

If you are using manure compost as bedding, you'll likely find the method mentioned above difficult because the bedding will start to dissolve and turn into mud or messy goop if you immerse it in water. Instead, approximate the amount of water to put in your bin by slowly adding water, a bit at a time, while stirring the bedding. Once all the bedding is just slightly damp, stop adding water. If you think you accidentally

Soak the bedding and then wring it out.

added too much water, add more dry bedding to absorb the excess.

Step 5: Fluffing it up

Wet bedding like shredded paper tends to clump, especially if you just squeezed it to wring out excess water. Worms need air to breathe, so break up any thick mats of bedding before you introduce the worms to their new home. A good way to ensure your bin bedding stays fluffy and doesn't mat is to use a combination of two types of bedding that have different shapes and textures. For example, mix some dead leaves, wood chips or straw in with the partly composted manure. The even mix of different types of bedding will prevent it from matting while providing variety to the worm's diet.

Step 6: Considering soil and other additives

Soil: Though composting worms do not need dirt to survive, a small sprinkling of soil in your bedding provides your worms with a bit of grit for their gizzards and eases digestion. The dirt also acts as a nice coating for moist paper bedding to prevent matting. Be careful not to add too much soil, and use it only as an additive, not as bedding; composting worms prefer to live above the soil in decaying matter. They will survive in soil, but it will be difficult to judge when the compost is ready because worm castings are similar in colour and texture to dirt. It is also difficult (if not impossible) to separate finished compost from dirt bedding. This is important if you are interested in

Fluff up your bedding so your worms have enough air.

breeding worms for fishing or for expanding your worm family.

Calcium carbonate: Another additive that increases the health of your worm bin is calcium carbonate, which is useful for balancing the pH of the bin if you are in the habit of putting in a lot of acidic wastes, such as coffee grounds or orange peels. The worms can use the calcium carbonate as grit for their gizzards, as well. You don't need a lot of calcium carbonate: a few spoonfuls per week should be enough. Worms prefer a slightly acidic environment, and too much calcium carbonate will turn the bin's pH alkaline, which is bad for the worms. Crushed eggshells do the same job as calcium carbonate, so you don't need to use calcium

carbonate if you are regularly adding crushed eggshells to the bin. **Warning:** slaked or hydrated lime is not appropriate for a worm bin and may kill the worms.

Rock dust: Also known as rock flour or aggregate crushing fines, rock dust is another great source of grit that adds micronutrients to the finished compost while increasing the health of your worms. Think of this additive as a multivitamin or health supplement; it is helpful but not necessary for your worms' survival—they will happily do their composting job as long as you are providing them with a balanced diet.

Adding Worms to Your Bin

Wait until your bin is ready for worms before you buy or acquire them. Check

A bit of soil eases your worms' digestion and prevents matting.

online for a local retail supplier, or contact a local garden centre or compost education centre. These suppliers will sometimes set you up with a bin that is already full of bedding and worms, so the only thing you need to do is feed the worms and harvest the finished compost. However, if you already have plans for the bin you want, you should be able to buy 500 g of worms in a bag (2500 worms). Worms eat half their weight in food per day, and they reproduce quickly, so unless you are running a commercial kitchen and need many worms right away, 500 g of worms should be enough. Find out the species of worm you are buying so you don't end up with one you don't want.

If you know someone who has a worm bin, you may not need to purchase any worms of your own. Worms repro-

duce quickly and will fill a bin to its capacity within a few weeks. You need only a few handfuls of worms (about as many as would fit in a medium sized margarine tub). Most people with worm composters are happy to give some worms away—especially at compost harvesting time. Inspect your friend's bin to make sure it is healthy, without contamination from flies or an overabundance of springtails, mites or pot worms, before you accept any worms (though if you don't mind a few tag-alongs and treat your bin kindly, you should be able to prevent their populations from getting out of control).

Transfer the worms within 24 hours to their new home if they were packaged with limited bedding and little food. Make sure the bag they are in has air holes so they can breathe.

Spread the worms on top of the bedding, and they will burrow into it.

To add your worms to their new home, spread them out on the top of the bedding and leave them exposed to light. The worms will burrow into the bedding to escape the light.

Feeding the Worms

In nature, composting worms are omnivores, eating both meat and vegetable matter. However, treat the worms in your bin like vegans and keep them on a restricted diet that does not include meat, eggs, milk products or fats. Provide them with foods that are full of carbohydrates, such as vegetable and fruit scraps and plain grain products. Unlike human vegans, the worms will eat waste kitchen scraps, coffee filters and tea bags, dust sweepings off the kitchen floor and crushed eggshells.

As long as the food has not been treated with harsh chemicals and is not coated with fatty oil or milk products, it should be okay for the worms to eat.

For quick composting, chop the waste so the worms have more surface area to feed on. The smaller you chop it, the faster they will eat it. You could even chop your waste with a food processor or blender to make it easier for the worms to eat. This is especially important for fruit and because the worms find it difficult to eat through tough skins. Depositing large fruit such as watermelon or squash in the bin might squish the worms.

For convenience, store your waste in a kitchen catcher before you feed it to the worms. Your kitchen catcher does

Chop up your waste for quicker composting.

not need to be large for a worm bin because you should feed and check on the worms every couple days (no less than once a week). If your kitchen catcher is small, you will empty it out more often and you can store it in the fridge or freezer until you empty it, if you so choose.

The Right Amount of Food

Worms eat half their weight in food a day, but they also reproduce quickly, so the number of worms you have in your bin can change along with how much you can feed them. You don't want to put too much food in a new bin, so you must figure out how much they can process so you know how much to feed them.

To figure out how much to feed your worms, start by using a grid system. Bury a bit of chopped food waste (250 mL) in one corner of the bin at least 5 cm under the surface of the bedding. The next day, look at the food and see how much the worms have eaten. If they have eaten most or all, bury a 250 mL portion beside the first bit of food you put in. If they have eaten very little of the food, or if it looks untouched, bury only 125 mL of new food next to the first bit. Every day or second day, check the food you put in to see how quickly it is being eaten, and

adjust your feeding portions appropriately. Following the grid pattern, place food in a new spot every time, starting from one end of the bin and working your way to the opposite end. If you started with only a small handful of worms donated from a friend, you will likely notice that the amount of food the worms eat increases over time, starting with the worms eating very little of what you put in to them eating voraciously after about one month. When you get past the final spot on the grid, check the first space you put food. If that food has not yet composted, wait until it has before you put in any new food.

Store excess food in the freezer or dispose of it until your worms catch up with your eating habits. After one month or so, the worms will be eating at full capacity. The bedding will start to disappear just as fast as the food, and it will be difficult to bury your food waste at least 5 cm under the surface. At this time, add more bedding to the surface of your bin, or you risk outbreaks of fruit flies and nasty smells.

> **Watermelon** is a wet, soft fruit that red wigglers love to eat more than any other food.

To cherish what remains of the earth and to foster its renewal is our only legitimate hope of survival.

–Wendell Berry

Common Food Items

Take a fairly common-sense approach when deciding what kind of kitchen waste to feed the worms. Ask yourself the following questions before you add the food to the bin.

- Has this item been treated with herbicides, pesticides, harsh cleaning agents or any other chemicals?
- Is this item oily or fatty?
- Is this item a milk product?
- Is this item a meat product?
- Is this item an inorganic substance that cannot break down in nature (i.e. metal, plastic, glass, rock)?

If you answered yes to any of these questions, do not put that item in your worm bin. The exception could be purchased fruits and vegetables from the grocery store that likely have been sprayed with chemicals. As long as the dose of these chemicals meets ratings that are acceptable for human consumption, they should be safe for the worms, as well. Most people rinse and clean vegetables and fruit before they eat them, and you should treat any scraps you are planning to feed the worms the same way.

Worm-friendly Wastes: a rough list

The following list is not comprehensive but should give you a rough idea of what you can put in the bin:

- all fruit and vegetable parts (peels, hearts, cores, fibres, etc.)
- beans (not in an oil sauce)
- coffee grounds and filters
- dead leaves from houseplants (not diseased)
- eggshells
- floor sweepings
- pizza crust

Worms love watermelon, but chop it up before adding it to your bin.

- plain breads (i.e. without jam and peanut butter)
- plain flour (this will mat easily, so put in only small amounts and mix it with other wastes or the bedding as you put it into the bin)
- plain oatmeal
- plain pasta
- rice (cooked or raw)
- simple, low-sugar cereals (e.g. Weetabix or Raisin Bran)
- tea leaves and bags
- used paper towel

It helps to know what some of the major food no-nos are for a worm bin. Although worms can eat some of these products without any adverse health effects, the foods' presence in the bin will cause smells and attract unwanted pests. Just think about your bin crawling with maggots or reeking of sour milk and you will understand why meat and milk are not good options. Oily products tend to break down slowly and can be harmful to the worms' health because it coats their skin and reduces their ability to breathe.

Bad Idea Foods: a rough list

The following list is not comprehensive but will give you a good idea of the types of items to avoid putting in your bin:

- chemically treated products (plants treated with pesticide, fungicide or herbicide, chemical fertilizers, paper towel soaked with cleaning agents, etc.)
- diseased items (infected plants and soil, tissues and paper towels from sick individuals, etc.)
- fats or oil products (food coated with salad dressing, margarine, peanut butter, cooking oil, etc.)
- hard-to-break-down items (seashells, wood, metal, plastic, glass, etc.)
- milk products (cheese, milk, butter, ice cream, yogourt, etc.)
- meat products (bones, blood, seafood, fish, raw or cooked eggs, etc.)
- sugar products (cake, chocolate, icing, frosted/sugary cereals, muffins, etc.)
- whole large fruits and vegetables (watermelon, sweet potatoes, etc.)

Do not add diseased items to your worm bin.

Maintaining Your Bin

Once the bin is established, you don't have to work hard to maintain it. There is no need to hover over it and check it everyday. The worms are sensitive to vibrations and don't appreciate you digging around in the bedding. Your duties to the bin are simple: feed the worms, monitor moisture levels and add bedding when necessary.

At first your worm bin will appear neat and orderly, and maintaining it will require little work from you other than feedings. After one month or so, the worms will have eaten some of their bedding, and it will be more difficult to bury the food, which may leave some of it exposed to the air. When you see this happening, it is time to add more bedding to the surface of the bin. Continue this practice until the compost is ready to harvest.

The life cycle of your bin involves building the bin, maintaining it and finally harvesting the compost. The number of worms you have, the amount of bedding you add and how frequently you feed the worms are all factors that affect the longevity of the life cycle of your bin.

Winter Worms

Though most people bring their worms indoors over winter, it is possible to build an insulated bin that your worms can live in outdoors. Keep in mind that if you do keep them outside, you will need to access the bin to feed the worms on a regular basis. Do not let your bin go below the freezing point,

or you risk killing all your worms. Be prepared to bring the worms in on cold nights; -30° C will freeze almost any insulated bin.

Tips for Warming the Winter Bin

- Make the bin at least 90 cm³ so that regular aerobic composting begins and raises the temperature of the pile during the cold winter months.
- Insulate your bin with styrofoam or straw bales to prevent heat from escaping.
- Purchase an electric immersion heater (like a bird bath heater) and place it in a sealed jug of water in the middle of your bin.
- Disturb your pile as little as possible because mixing it around releases heat into the air.

Harvesting the Compost

At some point you will need to take the finished compost out of the bin and prepare all new bedding for your worms. This process is called harvesting and it takes a bit of time and work. Several signs indicate when your bin is ready for harvesting. After a few months, the worms will have eaten all the bedding you originally put in the bin, and half the bin will be full of black, gooey earth. Your worms will decrease in number, and as time goes on, you will have more and more trouble finding adult worms in your bin.

The black gooey stuff is actually worm feces, known as worm castings. Worms cannot live in their own castings for long. So, as the concentration of castings rises, the number of worms decreases, starting with the adult worms. Worm breeders do not let their bins get to this stage; they constantly renew the bedding for their worms and separate the creatures from their castings as soon as possible. People who want finished compost let worm populations die down enough to make harvesting the compost worthwhile.

There are several ways to harvest the compost. Some ways require more effort than others. Your choice depends on how much time and energy you have. Regardless of the method you choose, time your harvesting so that most of the bedding has been converted to castings but a large population of worms still thrives.

Quick and Dirty

This method is popular with people who have an hour or two to spare and want to get harvesting over with as soon as possible.

- Transfer the contents of your bin onto a large, impermeable surface such as a garbage bag or driveway.
- Rebuild the bedding in the worm bin so that it is ready for a new population of worms.
- Take a handful of compost and pick out worms, cocoons, undigested bedding and food.
- Place the worms, etc., in the new bedding.
- Drop the castings into a bucket.

- Repeat until all the castings have been separated from the worms.

Quick and Cooperative

This method takes less time than the above method but requires a little more preparation.

- Take your bin outside on a sunny summer day (or use a bright light).
- Transfer the contents of your bin onto a large, impermeable surface.
- Rebuild your bedding in the worm bin so that it is ready for a new population of worms.
- Take the contents of your old bin and form it into little cones, 30 cm high.
- Make sure light shines on the cones. The worms will move away from the surface of the compost.
- Scoop the compost from the top of the cone and drop it into a bucket beside you.
- Reform the peak of the cone.
- Move to a new cone and repeat until the compost has been separated from the worms.
- Return the worms to the bin with new bedding.

Side to Side

This is a very popular method that requires little effort because the worms basically sort themselves.

- Shove the bin's contents to one side of the container.
- Build new bedding on the other side of the bin.

Side to side method

- For two weeks, feed the worms only on the side of the bin with new bedding. The worms should move over to that side.

- Remove the finished compost from the bin and place it in a pail.

- Fill the gap in the bin with new bedding.

- At this point, you can either pick stragglers out of the finished compost and return them to the bin, let the stragglers die in the pail or use the compost directly on your plants and give any stragglers the opportunity to tough it out in the soil or garden.

Dump or Die

Try this method if you don't want to bother waiting for the worms to sort themselves out.

- Remove the compost from the bin.

- Add new bedding.

- Scoop a few handfuls of worms from the bottom of the finished pile and put them in the new bedding.

- Throw the rest of the compost and worms in a pail and let it sit.

- Use the finished compost once all the worms are dead (2 to 3 months) or use the compost (worms and all) directly in the garden. The worms will do their best to survive until winter comes.

Worms' Best Buddies and Worst Enemies

Your worm bin is not a "members only" club in which only worms are allowed. Your worms actually have an entourage of decomposer buddies. A worm bin is an ecosystem that supports many decomposers feeding off each other and the food you give them. Some people freak out when they see mites, sow bugs and pot worms in their bin, but the worms need these helpers to break down their food so it is soft enough to eat.

Invisible Friends

Microorganisms: Actinomycetes, bacteria and fungi are present in soil and in compost piles. They are also at work in your fridge transforming the yogourt into a lumpy mess and on your bread, turning it green. These microscopic organisms enjoy the moist, dark environment of a worm bin and start breaking down your food scraps right away. The worms will eat them as well as the food they soften. Some people are allergic to certain moulds and fungi (or don't like to look at them flourishing in the bin); bury all food scraps under the surface of the bedding, and you won't have any problems.

Roundworms: Also referred to as nematodes, these microscopic worms break down decaying food. They are round and smooth and have a bad reputation among some worm breeders who worry that the roundworms will compete with red wigglers for food. However, you don't need to worry about controlling their numbers; the food gets broken down either way, and it doesn't really matter who eats it, as long as it gets eaten.

Bigger Bugs

If you grab a bit of decomposing food from your bin, you will likely see some critters crawling on it. Little white or reddish brown mites, pot worms, springtails and sow bugs are common. These organisms are no larger than 1 cm and are often smaller than 1 mm. Most of these decomposers either eat food wastes or feed on the excrement of other creatures in the bin. They often eat some of the microorganisms as well.

Pot worms: Also known as Enchytraeids, these little, white worms grow to no more than 1 cm in length and feed off the food waste in the bin. They are often mislabelled as nematodes (which are much smaller) or are mistaken for baby red wigglers. Pot worms thrive in acidic and wet bins. Though large numbers of pot worms help decompose the food in the bin, some people don't like how the bin looks when there are too many.

Sow bugs: These organisms are the largest critters in the bin (other than the worms), though they don't grow

Sow bug

larger than 1 cm in length. They are not actually bugs; they are isopods, which is another name for crustacean, like shrimp or crab. Sow bugs are also known as woodlice or slaters. The species that roll into a ball when threatened are referred to as pill bugs. They look like mini armadillos or, for those who know fossils, mini trilobites. These creatures have gills and need water to breathe. They feed on the waste food in the bin and prefer overly moist bins. Though they do not like to leave the moisture of the bin, they will feed on live, young plants if you house your worm bin in a nice, moist greenhouse.

Springtails: If you poke your finger in your bin, you might be surprised to see some small, white creatures jump away from your hand. Springtails earned their name because most can leap a few centimetres (somewhat like fleas). There are more than 1200 species of springtails, but not all of them can spring. Despite their ability to jump, springtails will stay in your bin, thriving in wet conditions and feeding on mould and decaying matter.

Mites: There are many different species of mites. About the size of a pinhead, they are difficult to see unless there are large numbers in your bin. They look like little moving round dots on the food and compost in your bin. Mites eat all sorts of stuff: fungi, mould, excrement, live plants, decaying matter, etc.

Only one species of mite is cause for concern in your bin: the earthworm mite. This mite is a parasite that clings to your worms and sucks their blood. It also pierces egg cocoons and sucks out the fluid. This reddish brown mite will not cause too many problems if it occurs in small numbers in your bin, but if its population explodes out of control, your worm population could be devastated.

Millipedes: Looking like worms with armour and lots of legs, millipedes are another type of decomposer in your bin. They have small heads, short antennae and hard-shelled bodies. Despite the name (meaning "thousand footed"), no millipedes have more than 500 legs, and most species have less than 200. They eat decaying matter and are important

Millipede

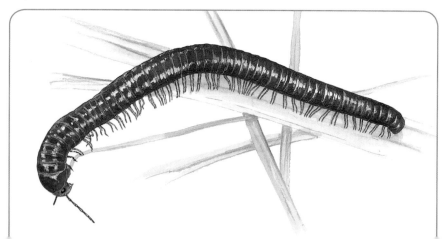

to the soil ecosystem. In Canada, there are around 60 species of millipedes; none are more than 8 cm long, and the most common species are usually less than 1 cm long.

Big Bullies

A few insects in soil are predatory toward worms and can kill off entire populations unless you are careful to destroy them as soon as you see them in your bin.

Centipedes: Unlike their decomposer cousins the millipedes, centipedes eat worms and live bugs. You can distinguish millipedes from centipedes by looking at the length of the antennae and legs. Millipedes have short antennae and many short legs; centipedes have fewer but longer legs and long antennae. Centipedes are nocturnal, so you may not see them often unless you disturb them when you are digging around in the bin. Although Canadian species of centipede are small like millipedes (no more than 8 cm long), the most common species are slightly longer (around 2.5 cm) than the most common millipedes.

Flatworms: Called tapeworms, planaria or turbellarians, these big, unsegmented worms will kill and eat your worms. Although they are nocturnal and rarely come to the soil's surface, they tend not to attack worms that live deep in the soil, preferring instead to feed on litter-dweller worms such as red wigglers. New Zealand and Australian flatworms are pests that have spread throughout Europe and decimated many earthworm populations all over Ireland. They have been found in the southern U.S., as well. These flatworms are not well adapted to our cold, northern climate, but they do nicely in a warm worm bin. They often hitch a ride in pots of exotic, imported plants, so if you plan to use the soil from imported plants in your worm bin, be sure to check it first for these critters. You can identify a flatworm by its size (6 to 30 cm long), slug-like appearance and glossy, dark skin. Watch for the eggs, as well. They look like black currants and range in size from 2 mm to 1 cm across.

Centipede

Troubleshooting

Every worm compost bin will have some sort of challenge for you to overcome. As you feed the worms, the environmental conditions (moisture, acidity, aeration, bug populations, etc.) change and have the potential to cause trouble. Luckily, the solution to most of these problems is fairly painless.

Bin Is Too Acidic

Worms like a slightly acidic bin but cannot survive in a pH below 5; they will try to escape a bin if the pH is too low. If you want to check your bin's pH, use a pH indicator probe or litmus paper, or make your own red cabbage pH test (see p. 16). The best way to adjust the pH is to stop adding acidic foods such as coffee grounds and orange peels and to remove any undigested acidic foods from the bin. Next,

Too much citrus waste could make your bin too acidic.

add crushed eggshells or sprinkle in 15 to 30 mL of calcium carbonate to bring the pH back up to a liveable level for the worms.

Bin Is Too Wet

If the bottom of your bin is more like a puddle of goop than a wrung-out sponge, your bin is too wet. You may have been overfeeding your worms, or your food choices may have included too much watermelon or fleshy fruit.

Most fruits and vegetables are 90 percent water, so when they break down, moisture levels in the bin rise. You may start to notice smells and anaerobic conditions near the bottom of your bin, especially if it is plastic with no air holes near the base.

If your bin is too moist, fluff up the bedding so air can reach the bottom, and add dry bedding to soak up some of the excess moisture. Alternatively, leave the lid off for a while so some of the moisture can evaporate—just be sure that food is not exposed at the surface.

The Worms Try to Escape the Bin

Your bin is an oasis in the dry, chemical-laden desert that is your house. None of the creatures in the bin should want to leave, so if you see them crawling up the sides and on the lid, something is wrong with your bin. Check to see if it is so wet that the worms are drowning or if it has turned too acidic. The bin might also be ready for harvesting. If all the bedding has been eaten and the worms are trying to escape, harvest the castings and rebuild the bedding.

Mould

Mould is another decomposer and is not detrimental to your bin. However, some people are allergic to mould spores or just don't like the look of mould on the surface of the bin. Mould occurs when food (particularly bread products) is left exposed on the surface of the bedding. To get rid of mould, turn the bedding so the mould and all food matter are under the surface.

Smells

Smells in a worm bin are usually caused either by anaerobic conditions or by food that is decomposing on the surface of the bedding. To prevent smells, you need to act like a cat in a litter box: bury your waste well below the surface of the bedding (at least 5 cm). Nasty smells can also result from putting inappropriate wastes, such as rotting meat or sour milk products, in the bin. Check the list of worm-friendly wastes (p. 122) if you are not sure what to feed your worms.

Anaerobic conditions are usually identified by the sour smell of methane and are caused by overfeeding and excess moisture. If you see a lot of undigested food in your bin, slow down or halt your feeding schedule until the worms have a chance to eat it, and add new dry bedding to fluff up what's in the bin. You could also try adding a new air hole or two to the side of the bin.

Sprouts

Sometimes potato peels, been sprouts and other seeded plants will begin to grow roots or send up shoots to the surface of your box. Even avocado pits can germinate a new plant. If you feel ambitious, transplant the sprout to its own pot or place it in your garden. Otherwise remove the germinating plant and chop it up to compost the bits again or heat these items in the microwave to kill them before you put them back in the bin.

If you add avocado pits to your bin, you may have to deal with sprouts.

Problem Pests

Ants

Ants like dry conditions and exposed, sugary food. Worm bins are usually fairly damp, so as long as you are burying your waste, the ants should stay away. If the bedding at the top of your bin is too dry, moisten it with a spray bottle.

See Appendix A (p. 149) for more information.

Fruit Flies

Most decomposers in your worm bin show up without invitation but do their best to stay inconspicuous while earning their place in the bin. The fruit fly, vinegar fly and fungus gnat didn't get that memo, and they do their best to multiply and swarm all over your bin, your house and in your face, if you let them.

Don't lose hope—there are ways to keep them out of your bin. If you stay vigilant and don't slack on your preventative duties, you can win the war against these little pests. A number of ways to prevent them from infesting your bin are listed below. You don't have to do all the methods mentioned; choose the ones that work best for you. If you don't take any preventative measures, you are asking for fruit fly trouble.

- Bury the waste at least 5 cm under the surface of the bedding in the bin. This is the most important preventative measure. Fruit flies are not burrowers, so they will not be able to reach the food and will leave the bin alone. Any flies that hatch in the food will not be able to reach the surface and will soon die. Even if this is the only preventative measure you take against fruit flies, you should still be successful. Add new bedding to the bin as the worms consume it so there is always enough to bury your food waste.

- Wash fruit and vegetable peels before feeding them to the worms. This may sound onerous, but most people wash and scrub fruits and vegetables

Take preventative measures against fruit flies.

before they eat them anyway. When you wash your peels, you wash away fruit fly eggs. Fruit flies lay their eggs in fruit peels often before the fruit reaches your home. The eggs are microscopic, so you won't know you have a possible infestation on you hands until it's too late.

- If you can't be bothered to wash your wastes, microwave them for at least one minute instead. The heat will likely kill all the eggs. Some people suggest freezing the wastes, but fruit flies survive freezing temperatures.

- Store your wastes in the fridge or freezer before you feed them to your worms so that any fruit flies already in your home can't lay eggs in the food. The flies can't get past the door seal, and if they do manage to sneak past you when you open the door, they'll go dormant in the cold and won't wake until they reach room temperature again.

- If you don't have room in the fridge for your wastes, use a finely screened compost pail to keep out flies. The pail should have a tight-fitting lid with pin-sized holes or a very fine screen to let in air and keep it aerobic.

- Use screening on the air holes of your bin to keep flies out or to keep swarms inside until you can vent the bin outside.

See Appendix A (p. 149) for more information about dealing with fruit fly infestations.

Bury, wash or microwave fruit wastes to prevent a fruit fly infestation.

I'm queen of my own compost heap, and I'm getting used to the smell.

–Ani DiFranco

Too Many Mites

Mites are helpful decomposers whose populations can get out of control in a bin. You can leave them be and allow their populations to fluctuate on their own. Large populations of mites develop when there is too much food in the bin or in acidic, overly moist or anaerobic conditions. They really like sweet, wet food. If you want to get rid of some mites, bait them with melon or squash rinds and toss the rinds in the trash once they are covered. Alternatively, place damp, whole sheets of newspaper on top of the bedding and remove and dispose of the sheets once mites have covered the bottom. Repeat the process until mite numbers reach acceptable numbers. Lastly, you could put the bin out in the sun with the lid off and let it dry out a little. Mites don't like sun.

Too Many Pot Worms

Pot worms are not hazardous to your bin and, in fact, help decompose your food. Their populations get out of control, however, when the bin is too wet or too acidic. Let the bin air out a bit or add more dry bedding to absorb the excess moisture. Cut back on feeding the worms citrus fruits or coffee grounds, and add more crushed eggshells.

Too Many Springtails

These little, white jumping bugs prefer moist environments, so if you don't like the look of too many of them in your bin, let it dry out a little. Remember, though, before you reduce their numbers, that they won't cause any harm and in fact contribute to decomposition.

Springtail

Using Finished Compost

Once you have separated the worm compost from the worms or finished producing a batch of aerobic or anaerobic compost, you will want to use the finished product. There are several ways to apply compost, such as incorporating it into the garden soil, using it as a side-dressing, top-dressing your lawn with it or using it for compost tea. How you use your compost depends on the volume of compost you produce and your needs. Before applying compost, be sure it is finished decomposing or you risk burning your plants or pulling nitrogen away from the soil and plants.

Is Your Compost Ready?

Finished compost is dark and crumbly. The original feedstock should be unrecognizable—you may notice a few fibres or bits of original feedstock, but most of the material will have decayed into a dark, dirt-like matter. Finished compost can be rough and multi-textured, but when you put it through a screen it should crumble to look like dark soil.

Finished worm compost is very moist and consequently is difficult to screen. As long as it is dark and looks mostly like dirt, it can be used right away with your plants.

Make sure your compost is ready before you add it to your garden.

Anaerobic compost is usually quite wet and acidic. Before it can be applied, it needs to air out for at least few months to kill the anaerobes and lose some of the excess moisture. A general rule is to use anaerobic compost one year from the date you started the composting process.

Aerobic compost generally needs to be cured before it can be used.

Curing Aerobic Compost

To cure aerobic compost, let it sit for about one to six months. This is especially important for hot aerobic compost that was produced in less than one month. The decomposers in this process are revved up and ready to eat, so you have to give them time to settle down a bit.

Once the temperature at the centre of the pile has lowered and stabilized, check to see if the compost is ready to be used in the garden. The easiest way to test the readiness of your compost is to place it in an airtight plastic bag or bucket and let it sit for a day or two. If the compost smells like sweet dirt and is relatively unchanged when you open the bag, it is safe to use on your plants. If it smells rotten or like ammonia, it still has active decomposers and is not finished curing. Let the whole pile sit and test it again in a week.

The best time to use aerobic compost in your garden is at the end of the growing season when you are preparing your garden for winter or in early spring two to three weeks before planting. Applying the compost to the soil before introducing new plants allows the decomposers time to adjust to their new environment and finish curing completely. Any nitrogen taken from the soil by the decomposers will be returned once the decomposers have completed the curing process.

Killing Weeds and Seeds

Seeded weeds do not belong in a cold compost pile. If you do accidentally put weed seeds in a cold pile, some of the seeds will probably survive the composting process. Fortunately there are a few ways to kill the seeds off.

One way to prevent spreading the weeds around your garden is to put the compost in a lidded, aerated container, moisten the compost and let the seeds germinate. Pull the plants out and put them in the garbage (or a new compost pile). Turn the compost to bring new seeds to the surface, and repeat the process until no new seeds germinate.

If you don't want to wait for the weeds to germinate, try pasteurizing the compost. Pasteurizing will kill most weeds and soil diseases; however, it also kills the beneficial bacteria in the soil. The beneficial bacteria make compost nutrients available to your plants, so

pasteurizing will degrade the quality of your compost.

The easiest way to pasteurize is to use the heat of the sun. Set your moistened compost under a clear plastic sheet in a sunny location for at least one month. You can set up an aluminum foil wall beside your pile to double the amount of light hitting the plastic, which will intensify the heat.

If you want to pasteurize compost quickly, lightly moisten it and throw a layer (no more than 10 cm deep) in an oven bag, a roasting pan or a casserole dish. Cook the compost in a barbeque or oven until it reaches 180° C for at least half an hour. Use a meat thermometer to measure the temperature. Baking compost in the oven can smell unpleasant, so you are better off pasteurizing outdoors, if possible.

Screening

You don't need to screen your compost if you plan on digging it into the garden. But, if you like the look of a uniform, dirt-like compost, you can screen the finished compost before

Kill any weeds and weed seeds in your compost to avoid spreading the weeds to your garden.

you use it. Screening sifts out undigested feedstocks and breaks down lumps and clumps into a nice crumbly mix. Screening is a good idea if you plan on using the compost as a side-dressing or mulch in a decorative garden or in potted plants. If you plan to use compost as a top-dressing for your lawn, you will definitely need to screen it first.

You can construct your own compost screen by purchasing 12 mm metal screen or mesh and stapling it to a square wood frame. A 6 mm screen can be used to produce a fine compost product, but it may get clogged up if the compost is moist. Generally, you should make sure your compost is dry before you attempt screening.

You can construct your own screen.

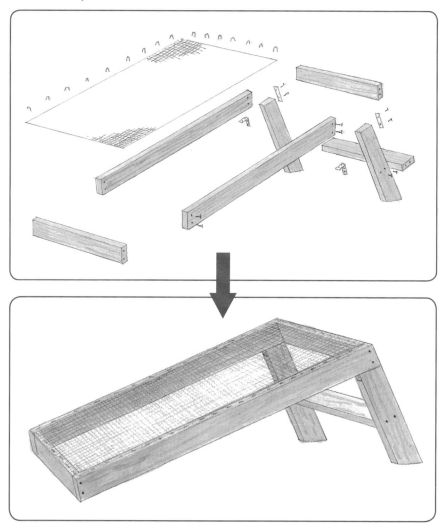

Storing Compost

If you want to keep your compost for an extended period of time, you should, at the very least, cover it with a tarp to protect it from the elements. Ideally, however, the compost should be contained, covered and aerated. Containing and covering the compost prevents nutrients from leaching out of the pile into the ground below and protects the compost from rain and from weed seeds blowing in the wind. Aerating the pile ensures the beneficial bacteria will survive. Aerate the compost by leaving air holes in the container and stirring the compost once a month or by placing a perforated pipe through the middle of the pile.

Using Compost in the Garden

Digging In

In new gardens, mix a 2.5 cm layer of compost 7.5 to 10 cm deep into your soil at least two weeks before planting

This Toronto Zoo garden has benefited from the addition of composted animal manure.

your garden. Add the compost in after you've applied your regular organic fertilizer treatment.

For established gardens, you will need to add only a 1.25 cm layer of compost once a year. You can dig the compost into the soil using a hoe, shovel or rototiller or by using a soil turning method called double-digging.

Double-digging is a labour intensive process that involves digging a trench to the depth of your shovel and using a garden fork to loosen the soil at the bottom of the trench, then replacing the original soil, which has been mixed with compost.

Using a rototiller makes digging compost into the soil easy and aerates the soil in the process. However, many gardeners are turning to double-digging instead of rototilling because they are concerned that their subsoil may become hard packed from overuse of the roto-tiller. The weight of the machine compacts the soil below the level reached by the blades, and this hard-packed layer

Digging compost into the soil can be a labour intensive.

Try to keep rototilling to a minimum to avoid damaging the soil structure.

limits plants from establishing deep root systems. The blades of a rototiller can also damage the soil ecosystem.

If you don't dig the compost into the soil at least two weeks before you plan to plant seeds, you should wait until the seeds have established as seedlings and then apply the compost as a side-dressing. This is especially important for lettuce and some other vegetable seeds that are vulnerable to decomposers.

Mulch

If you have an abundance of fresh compost, you can use it as a mulch. A layer of fresh, uncured compost, 5 to 7.5 cm thick, will act as an effective weed suppressant in your garden and raised beds while providing water retention and nutrients to the soil. Leave 2.5 cm of space between the compost and the base of plant stems to avoid burning the plants.

Side-dressing

If you don't have enough compost to cover your entire garden with a 2.5 cm thick layer, or if you produce compost mid-way through the growing season, you can feed established perennial plants, shrubs and trees with a compost side-dressing.

Place a 15 cm thick layer of completely cured compost around the base of each plant to the edge of the drip line. Leave 2.5 cm of space between the compost and the stem of the plant. Don't bother digging compost into the soil—you risk damaging the plant's root.system. Water, worms and other soil organisms will ensure that the compost eventually makes its way below the surface of the soil to the plant's roots.

When applying compost as a side-dressing, spread it around the base of the plant out to the drip line.

Top-dressing

For established pots or gardens, you can use compost as a top-dressing to help them grow. Layer the moist compost 5 mm deep on the surface of the soil in your pot. Place the compost around (not directly on) the base or stem of the plant. Make sure the pot has decent drainage to wash away excess salt. Do not water plants with water that has been treated with softener because the salt concentrations could damage their growth. For garden plants (not in a pot or container), place the compost underneath the area covered by the leaves of the plant. Water dripping off of the leaves will gradually cause nutrients from the compost to trickle down into the soil and roots. Top-dress your plants every six to eight weeks.

Lawn Care

Compost can be part of your lawn care program. Mix compost into the soil before laying down new sod or spreading seed. The compost will help your grass develop an extensive root system and will prevent weeds from establishing in the lawn.

Spread compost in a thin layer over your entire lawn (above & below).

Incorporate compost into the soil of established lawns by top-dressing with finely screened compost. Spread the compost with a fertilizer spreader or by raking out an even 5 mm layer of compost over the lawn. Aerate the lawn before spreading the compost to ensure deeper penetration of the compost into the soil and to improve the health of the soil and grass root structure.

Transplants

Use a bit of compost to help establish new plants and seedlings directly where they are planted. If you are putting in new annual plants, such as tomatoes, or even new perennials, such as rhubarb or raspberries, toss a little compost in and around the hole before you put in the plant. The compost will help the plant recover from the shock of being transplanted. You can side-dress the plants again with compost later in the growing season.

When putting in new trees or shrubs, do not put compost in the hole. Instead, side-dress the tree so that it is forced to spread its roots to look for nutrients beyond the area where it was planted.

Work the compost into the lawn using a rake or broom (above & below)

Use worm compost in small concentrations in your garden and containers.

Worm Compost

You don't have to dry out or screen worm compost before you use it because a lot of the beneficial properties exist in the compost only when it is moist and full of life and decaying matter. Even when it is full of worms, the compost can be added to your soil. The worms and their decomposer buddies won't eat live plants and will contribute further to the health of the soil.

Worm castings are more potent than compost made in your backyard composter. The castings are high in nitrogen, phosphorous, potassium and many micronutrients. Most importantly, worm castings are full of microorganisms and humic acid, the stuff that makes the nutrients stored in organic compounds available to plants as food.

When you harvest the compost from your bin, it may only produce a small amount of finished compost. Thankfully, only a little bit of vermicompost is necessary in a pot or garden to be beneficial.

Garden Mix

The ideal ratio for topsoil to worm castings is 5:1. Though you can use larger concentrations of vermicompost on your plants or garden, too much may harm the plants because of high salt content. With proper drainage, the salt should wash away shortly after the first few times you water your plants.

When preparing new pots for transplantation, you can premix the worm castings with your potting soil blend and use that mix to fill your pots.

In the garden, sprinkle small amounts of the compost into seed rows or in the holes where you will be planting.

Experiment with a compost mix in your containers.

Using Compost in Containers

Using compost in pots and containers is a topic of heated debate in the gardening community. Many books encourage the use of a mixture composed of one-third compost, one-third sand and one-third potting soil mix for houseplants and to grow seedlings. Contemporary gardening experts now suggest using soil-less mixes of bark chips and crushed granite with an intense chemical fertilizer and watering treatment instead.

Proponents of using compost in planters point out that it does not involve using non-renewable supplies to feed houseplants, and it cuts down on fertilizer pollution in the sewer lines.

Advocates of the use of soil-less mixes argue that bacteria and drainage do not behave in containers as they do in the garden. Drainage and aeration is a big issue for containers, which do not benefit from the wicking effect of the garden subsoil. Container plants are also more prone to soil diseases and insect infestations; soil-less mixes eliminate all bacteria life to prevent harming the plant. When using a soil-less mix, you cannot rely on bacteria to feed the plants, so you have to water plants with a consistent fertilizer treatment program.

You can decide which program is best for your houseplants. Experiment by planting a few plants with your own homemade compost mix and a few other plants with a homemade soil-less mix. After a year, you should know which container gardening system you prefer, and you can repot your plants appropriately.

Other Compost Uses

Compost Inoculant

If you plan to build a new compost pile, you can store some of the finished compost from your last batch to inoculate your new pile. Just sprinkle a little finished compost throughout the new pile as you build it. Although your compost pile and garden soil already contain composting bacteria, inoculating the pile increases the amount of composting bacteria in the new pile, giving it a head start.

Compost Tea

Compost tea is a great source of nutrients and beneficial bacteria for your plants and soil. When it is applied to foliage, the beneficial bacteria suppress and kill disease organisms. When applied to the soil around the plants, compost tea increases the soil fertility and releases more nutrients to your plants. There are two ways to make your own liquid fertilizer using compost.

Traditional Tea Recipe

The method that has been used for years by gardening enthusiasts is to steep compost in a burlap sack, old sock or cheesecloth in a clean container.

Instructions:

1. Fill an old rain barrel, 20 L bucket or watering can with water. If you are using chlorinated municipal water, let the water sit for at least 24 hours so the chlorine evaporates out, or treat it with an aquarium dechlorinator solution.

2. Add compost to the sack or cloth and drop it in the container, letting it soak for two to three days. Stir the tea at least once a day.

3. Once the compost tea has reached a pale yellow colour (like weak tea), remove the compost sack from the container and use the tea on your plants.

4. Reuse the compost sack until it no longer changes the colour of the water.

5. Mix the spent compost back into an active pile or dig it into the garden

Let us give Nature a chance; she knows her business better than we do.

–Michel Eyquen de Montaigne

Modern Aeration Tea Recipe

Some compost tea enthusiasts have developed another way to make super compost tea. They incorporate intense aeration techniques to ensure the beneficial aerobic bacteria prosper and breed in the water and to discourage the development of anaerobic bacteria that naturally develop in watery environments. For this method, you will need a 20 L bucket, an aquarium air pump, cheesecloth, molasses, lemon juice, fresh compost and dechlorinated water.

Instructions:

1. First, set up the air pump with an extension of aquarium tubing that is long enough to reach the bottom of the bucket. For extra aeration, use a gang valve and multiple tubes. Anchor the tubing in place using a weighted object, such as a rock.
2. Put a shovelful of compost in the bucket and fill the bucket with dechlorinated water.
3. To feed the bacteria, add 30 mL of unsulphured molasses and 15 mL of lemon juice.
4. Run the pump for two days, making sure you stir the mixture at least once per day.
5. Before the end of the second day, screen the compost through cheesecloth or another porous fabric. You can now either use the compost tea directly on your plants or dilute it with more dechlorinated water until it reaches a pale yellow colour. Use the compost tea right away to get the full benefit of the bacteria.

→ **Warning**: Do not use manure or manure compost to make compost tea or you risk spreading pathogens like *E. coli* and salmonella in your garden.

→ **Tip**: If you don't want to make your own tea system, compost tea brewing kits are available for purchase at many garden centres and farming supply stores.

Buying Compost

Home compost is not always ready when we need it or available in the quantities that we want. Many organic gardeners have turned to supplementing their supply of compost with a commercially available product. Fortunately, there are a variety of suppliers ready to sell the compost at a reasonable price.

Municipal Compost

Does your local municipality have a green waste collection program? If so, it most likely has a supply of compost for sale. Before buying municipal or commercial compost, you should investigate the processing method that was used to make the compost and inquire about testing policies and adherence to regulations. Because the feedstock for municipal compost is likely contaminated with weeds, pesticides and diseases, most municipalities use hot composting to achieve the high heat levels required to kill pathogens and weed seeds; they also rigorously test the grade of their compost. As a branch of a government agency, municipal compost operations are kept under the regulatory agency microscope, and their product will have use restrictions if they don't meet the required safe-use standards. Therefore, as a general rule, most municipal composts available for sale without use restrictions are likely safe to use.

If you are not sure that the compost is safe, buy a small sample and test it in an unused corner of your garden. If you find after a week that an unusual type of weed is popping up or if the test seeds and plants that you put in the soil die or don't germinate, you might not want to use that particular brand of compost.

Tip: Not all commercial compost suppliers are tested or regulated as vigorously as municipal suppliers. Be sure to research and test commercial composts before using them throughout your garden.

Mushroom Compost

Mushrooms are categorized as decomposers. Mushroom farmers grow their crops on a rich compost mix of straw and animal manures. Once the mushrooms have taken what they need from the decomposing manures and straw, the decomposed matter (i.e. compost) is removed and is available for sale as mushroom compost.

Mushroom compost has not finished curing and can almost be considered an organic fertilizer. It is potent, so use only a 10 percent application to your soil or garden, or you risk burning your plants and killing them. In other words, instead of using a 2.5 cm thick application of compost around your garden, use only a 1 cm application instead. When used sparingly, mushroom compost is a great addition to any garden.

Appendix A: Problem Pests

Unwelcome Insects

Ants

Ants are decomposers and help break down food. However, they can become pests, and red ants bite. Ants really like dry, undisturbed piles with sugary treats in them—the usual condition of many cold compost piles.

For aerobic piles, the solution to your ant problem is to water the compost pile and mix it. Sweet fruit, such as grapes and bananas, have the potential to attract ants. Bury the fruit under dry, brown wastes to make it less accessible. Try elevating your compost bin on a pallet or legs so ants don't make a home in the bin. Place the legs of the bin in a water or oil bath to cut off the creatures' access to the pile.

Consider treating the pile with natural deterrents. Spread a thick band of gooey stuff, such as petroleum jelly, around the bin. Ants also hate cucumbers, mint tea leaves, cayenne pepper, lemon juice, cinnamon, coffee grounds and garlic. Use these items to make a natural barrier that the ants will not cross. Make sure there are no bridges, such as fallen debris, that the ants can use to get over the barrier.

Ants don't like moist environments, so if you have an ant problem in your anaerobic composter, your pile is too dry. Make sure the pile is packed tight with no airspaces, and water it thoroughly.

Another way to prevent ants from visiting your pile is to destroy their colony. Pour at least 4 L of boiling or soapy water on the anthill while mixing it in with a shovel or stick. As a last resort you could use an ant poison, such as boric acid, Logic or Amdro. You do not want to kill the beneficial decomposers in your pile, so don't put these items directly in your compost bin; instead, put them near the anthill.

Ant

Fruit fly

Flies

It is normal to have a few flies buzzing around a compost pile, especially if you are putting in kitchen wastes. The best way to prevent or fix a large fly problem in an aerobic compost bin is to bury food wastes under at least 5 cm of dry, brown wastes and cover them with a thin layer of dirt.

With anaerobic composting, the decomposing matter is likely too dry if you have a fruit fly infestation. Water the pile thoroughly and cover it with 5 cm of dirt, and don't open the lid more than once a week if it is a pit composter or big barrel system. Don't try to kill flies using pesticides or you will kill the anaerobes. Consider transforming the pit or barrel into a batch anaerobic system by not opening the bin for a few months, which will ensure the flies die out.

Fruit Fly Infestations with Indoor Composters

The most common way to attract fruit flies to your bin is by leaving food exposed at the surface. To get rid of the flies, you can do several things. First, when you first suspect flies are in your bin (if you see a couple of them escaping the bin or on the lid), take the bin outside BEFORE YOU OPEN THE LID. Even in -30° C weather, take your bin outside your home or business. Let the first swarm pass out of the bin into the outside air.

With a worm composter, leave the bin outside with the lid off and go get some bedding. Put damp bedding on the surface of the bin (at least 5 cm everywhere), making sure no food is exposed. Put a dish or jar of apple cider vinegar (or white vinegar with a little sugar dissolved in it) in the bin on the surface of the bedding and put the lid back on. In spring, summer or autumn, leave the bin outside; in winter, bring it back indoors. Now don't open the lid for one week. When you are ready to look again, repeat the steps above, starting with taking your bin back outside.

If the swarm was released in your house, create flytraps by placing saucers of beer or vinegar, cone traps (described below) or fly paper around your house. Be sure to store your kitchen catcher in the fridge or freezer until the fly population is under control.

Cone trap

Apple cider vinegar trap

A cone trap is made by cutting and stuffing the corner of a resealable plastic bag into a small homemade cone, such as the neck of a plastic ketchup bottle. Fold the top of the bag over the lip of the cone and secure the bag with an elastic band. Fill the bottom of the plastic bag with apple cider (or beer) and some rotten apple and seal the bag. Suspend the trap in an area where the concentration of flies is highest. The flies will be attracted to the cider and fly into the bag, where they will be trapped, eventually drowning in the cider.

Change the liquid when it gets too full of flies (every couple of days). Be sure to squish the flies, because they sometimes dry out and can fly out of the drain after you wash them down.

Slug

Slugs

Slugs are common critters in many climates. They prefer the cool, moist, dark, covered locations provided by organic mulches and comforter compost piles. They eat fresh waste, pet feces and young, leafy plants. Slugs eat quickly and can destroy entire plants in an evening.

The best way to protect your garden plants is to use rough-surfaced mulches, such as gravel or bark, around the base of your plants. Slugs don't like moving over rough surfaces. You can also place barriers around your plants or beds to prevent slugs from getting too close. Pet fur and human hair stick to and dry out sensitive slug skin and will drive slugs crazy; therefore, the slugs will avoid barriers made from hair and fur. You can also make your own pointy edged, 10 cm high, hardware cloth mini fences and place them around your plants to keep the slugs away.

If slugs are causing a lot of trouble, trap them or manually pick them out of your garden or comforter compost pile. Place a fermenting yeasty liquid like beer in a bowl, and partially bury the bowl so that the lip is level with the soil. The slugs will fall in and drown. To trap them, place a sheet of plywood in the garden, and in the cool early morning, go out and collect the slugs that accumulate under the board and place them in a saltwater bath to kill them.

Yellow Jackets

Most wasps and bees are beneficial and prey on pest insects that harm your garden. The nasty ones that like to sting you are called yellow jackets. Cold compost bins sometimes attract wasps.

Yellow jacket

If a pile is not stirred and is a bit dry, wasps will make a home in it. To prevent wasps from getting too comfortable in your pile, poke it (even ever-producing piles) regularly with an aerator device and keep the pile moist. The wasps will settle somewhere else that isn't so busy.

Another thing to consider is that wasps especially like sweet foods, such as fruit rinds that are left uncovered on top of the pile. Cover the foods with dry, brown dry materials and a little dirt so wasps are not attracted to the pile in the first place.

If wasps have already made a home in your bin, try feeding the pile in the evening when they start to settle down. Don't bother with traps—wasps reproduce faster than you can kill them.

If the bin is in an out-of-the-way location, you can leave it alone all season. When frost comes on in winter, bundle up in layers of clothing with no skin exposed. Dig into the pile (wasps are dormant in winter and are therefore drowsy), remove the wasp nest and drown it in a bucket of water. After removing the nest, soak the pile with water. Any remaining wasps will die when the pile turns into a big icicle. You can deconstruct the pile in spring and start over in a new area, being sure to take preventative action against wasps this time round.

Another option is to set out a shallow dish in spring with 2.5 cm of sugar water and a little detergent in it. The queen will emerge to feed after winter and drown in the water. Wasp poison known as microencapsulated diazinon or Knox-Out 2FM can be mixed with tuna or cat food and placed in a trap. The workers will share this high-protein bait with the queen and larvae, and the nest should start to die within a week. Keep the bait away from children and house pets because they can be seriously injured or killed if they consume it.

As a last resort, you can call a professional pest control agent to get rid of the wasps. Only hire agents who have a special vacuum to suck up the wasps. Chemical sprays will kill all the creatures in your pile and will make the compost unsafe to use on your garden.

Mischievous Mammals

Bears

Bears are found throughout many northern, forested or mountainous areas in Canada. Almost every province or territory has at least a few roaming around, and not just in rural areas; bears have been known to wander into urban

Take steps to avoid attracting bears to your yard.

areas, as well. The best way to keep them away from your composter is prevention—once a bear has found your yard, it will likely come back on a regular basis to check for food. Don't put any kitchen scraps in your bin if you are concerned about bears, especially not meat, eggs, cooked foods, pastas, breads, cereals, pet foods, milk products or fats. Try an indoor composting method like worm composting or anaerobic composting instead for those wastes. Bears are not attracted to decomposing plant wastes, such as leaves or grass, so you can safely add them to your outdoor compost bin.

Raccoons

Some people like raccoons and don't mind when they dig in the pile (free aeration labour). However, raccoons can make quite a mess and will not restrict themselves to the pile. They might start eating the veggies in your garden, too. These cute, clever little

Raccoon

buggers can get into almost any compost bin that does not have a locking lid (and even some that do). Their noses are really sensitive, and they can even find food buried deep in a compost pile.

If you have raccoons in your area, you can do several things to keep them out of your bin. First, you can choose to compost only yard wastes and keep kitchen wastes in an indoor unit like a worm bin. Raccoons also like to eat worms and grubs, so they may still visit your pile where worms and grubs congregate. However, the absence of smelly, tasty foods will ensure they will not target your pile or yard right away.

Perhaps the best solution is to purchase or construct a sturdy compost bin with a locking lid and doors that the raccoons can't open. You should still keep the really tasty treats (breads, pastas, cereals, pet foods, etc) out of your pile.

Finally, if raccoons insist on visiting your yard and you have trouble keeping them out of your bin, you can contact your local pest control agency to live trap them and remove them from the area.

Rats, Mice and Burrowing Animals

Moles, gophers, rats and mice all have the ability to dig underneath your bin and access the pile from below. Even some of the bigger ground dwellers will try to dig a trench to get at the bottom of your pile. Whereas moles, skunks and raccoons will only feed on the worms and decomposers in your pile, rats and mice might make a home.

One way to prevent pests from nesting in your bin is to poke it and stir it weekly and make sure it stays moist. Mice and rats don't appreciate the activity or the moisture and will go somewhere else to live. In winter, when the pile cools off but stays a few degrees warmer than its surroundings, it can be difficult to keep the animals away, but at least they are not nesting in your basement, garage or house.

The best way to prevent these critters from accessing your pile is to build it on top of wire mesh or hardware cloth with a grid no larger than 12 mm^2 and no smaller than 6 mm^2 so worms and larger decomposers still have access to the pile from below. Do not use chicken wire because mice can chew right through it. Stake the bin to the ground so there is no room for them to squeeze between the edge of the bin and the mesh. A fully enclosed bin also prevents these small animals from accessing your pile. If you enclose your bin, make sure the bottom has some small holes for drainage and ventilation.

Rat

Appendix B: Understanding Soil Structure

Your soil's ability to hold water and air depends largely on its structure. Soil is mostly made up of inorganic matter (95 percent), which is essentially little pieces of rocks and minerals. The texture of your soil depends on the variety of particle sizes it contains; sand has particles smaller than 2 mm, silt has particles smaller than 0.5 mm and clay has particles smaller than 0.002 mm. You might find it difficult to grow plants in your soil if it contains more than its fair share of any one of these three particle types. For example, if the soil is too sandy, you will have to water more often because water retention will be an issue. If the soil has too much clay, you will have trouble getting enough air to the plant roots and bacteria that live in the soil. Clayey soil drains poorly but is also hard to work with when it dries out and turns as hard as cement. Loam is soil that contains a good mix of sand, clay and silt; it is the best soil for growing most plants.

If you are unsure of your garden's soil type, you can do a simple test. Grab a handful of moist soil and squeeze it

Loam

(add some water if it is too dry, but not so much that you make it muddy). If, when you open your hand, the soil breaks apart or crumbles, you have sandy soil. If the soil stays in a ball, pinch and flatten it with your thumb, letting it hang a bit from your fist. If it falls from your hand before it stretches more than 2.5 cm, you have a sandy or silty loam. If it feels both gritty and smooth, it's loam. If it can stretch up to 5 cm, you have a silty or clayey loam, and if it hangs on for longer than 5 cm, you have clayey soil. If it feels gritty, it is a sandy clay. If it feels smooth, you have clay.

Soil type is largely influenced by the region in which you live and the geological history of the area. Was your area carved out by glaciers? Was it the flood plain of an ancient river, or perhaps the bed of an ancient sea? Was it a wetland drained by developers before you moved in, or a forest logged by settlers hundreds of years ago? These factors can influence the type of soil you find in your backyard. So although it is nice to know what kind of soil you have, you often can't do much about it. It can be very taxing (and expensive) to try to add the correct quantity of sand, silt or clay to alter your garden's soil structure. Regardless of the soil type in your yard, the best solution is to add compost—it will aggregate a sandy soil so that it retains water or create air pockets and loosen up a clayey soil.

Clay

Glossary

Acid: a substance that has a rating lower than 7 on the pH scale

Actinomycetes: decomposer microbes that produce humus during the later stages of the composting process

Activator: a substance that claims to increase the heat, speed of decomposition or nutrient value in your compost pile

Aeration composting: composting method that keeps air in the pile so aerobic decomposers (aerobes) will thrive

Aerobes: bacteria that require air to survive

Alkaline: a substance that has a rating higher than 7 on the pH scale

Anaerobes: bacteria that thrive in airless environments

Browns: dead and dry waste feedstocks (e.g. brown leaves or straw) that are high in carbon

Cold composting: a method of aeration composting that does not heat up beyond the temperature range required for mesophilic bacteria to thrive

Compost: the decayed organic matter that results from the act of composting; usually dark, crumbly and dirtlike in appearance

Compost tea: liquid fertilizer high in bacteria and nutrients made from soaking compost in water

Decomposers: any organisms that participate in the decomposition process (from insects to bacteria)

Feedstock: any substance you put in your compost pile

Greens: fresh waste feedstocks (e.g. grass clippings or kitchen scraps) that are high in nitrogen

Hot composting: a method of aeration composting that heats up to the temperature range required for thermophilic bacteria to thrive

Humus: decomposed organic matter or compost

Innoculant: a material of high microbial content added to a compost pile to introduce a particular type of decomposer or to increase microbial activity

Inorganic: any substance that was not once part of a living organism (e.g. a chemical or mineral)

Leaf mould: compost made from rotted leaves

Mesophiles: decomposer bacteria that flourish in temperatures between 10° and 45°C

Mushroom compost: a mostly decomposed mixture of straw and manure leftover from mushroom farming

Organic: any substance that is or once was part of a living organism

Pathogen: strain of bacteria that can be harmful to humans

pH: a unit of measurement for acidity and alkalinity on a scale that ranges between 1 and 14, where 7 is neutral, lower than 7 is acidic and higher than 7 is alkaline

Psychrophiles: decomposer bacteria that flourish in temperatures between -10° and 20° C

Soil conditioner: a substance (such as compost) that adds both micro- and macro-nutrients to the soil but is not high enough in potassium, nitrogen or phosphorus to be qualified as a fertilizer

Thermophiles: decomposer bacteria that flourish in temperatures between 40° and 70° C.

Vermicompost: compost made from the feces of worms

Worm castings: feces of worms

References and Suggested Further Reading

Appelhof, Mary. *Worms Eat My Garbage*. 2nd ed. Kalamazoo, MI: Flower Press, 1997.

Ball, Jeff and Robert Kourik. *Easy Composting*. San Ramon, CA: Ortho Books, 1992.

Ball, Liz. *Smith & Hawken: Hands-on Gardener: Composting*. New York: Workman Publishing, 1997.

Bradley, Fern Marshall, *et al*. Eds. *Rodale Organic Gardenning Basics: Soil*. Vol. 2. Emmaus, PA: Rodale Press, 2000.

Campbell, Stu. *Let it Rot! The Gardener's Guide to Composting*. Pownal, VT: Storey Communications, 1975.

Cullen, Mark and Lorraine Johnson. *The Real Dirt*. Toronto: Penguin Books, 1992.

Fish, Kathleen DeVanna, *et al*. Eds. *Rodale Organic Gardenning Basics: Compost*. Vol. 8. Emmaus, PA: Rodale Press, 2001.

Francis, Robert. *The Complete Book of Compost*. New York: Berkley Books, 1998.

Gershuny, Grace. *Start with the Soil*. Emmaus, PA: Rodale Press, 1993.

Hart, Rhonda Massingham. *Bugs, Slugs & Other Thugs*. Pownal, VT: Storey Communications, 1991.

Martin, Deborah L. and Grace Gershuny. Eds. *The Rodale Book of Composting*. Emmaus, PA: Rodale Press, 1992.

Pleasant, Barbara and Deborah L. Martin. *The Complete Compost Gardening Guide*. North Adams, MA: Storey Publishing, 2008.

Roulac, John W. and Marialyce Pedersen. Eds. *Backyard Composting*. Ojai, CA: Harmonious Technologies, 1994.

About the Author

SUZANNE LEWIS
has a decade's experience in educating the public about composting and waste reduction for the City of Edmonton. She has a degree in English and Media Studies from the University of Alberta and a professional writing diploma from MacEwan College. Suzanne practises what she preaches—she commutes to work by bicycle or takes the bus, and she always reuses and reduces before she recycles.